MAY YOU ALWAYS FIND THE
HUMOR IN LIFE,
AND NEVER FORGET TO LAUGH
OUT LOUD!

XO,

Lee

2019

BLACK SHEEP TRIES BLEACH

humorous stories to ease
life's growing pains

LEE VOLPE

First Edition: December 2017

Printed in the United States of America

ISBN: 978-1-939237-55-2

Published by Suncoast Digital Press, Inc.
Sarasota, Florida, USA

Cover photo by H photography

Special thanks to Miss Margie's Farm
(Eagle River, WI) and to Pepper (cover model)

Dedication

Mommy and me (1977)

For my Mommy,

who has always believed, encouraged, and supported me.

You were my first fan and continue to be my loudest cheerleader.

Thank you for always seeing ME, even when I would lose sight of myself.

— MORE. xo

For those who think they can't and the ones who believed they could

I dedicate this book to you!

Table of Contents

Preface

The Storyteller...(Me)

Growing up, I always heard, "If it's going to happen, it will happen to Lee." True as this statement has proven to be, I believe it all happened to ME, so I could share it with YOU.

Black Sheep Tries Bleach is the modern-day survival guide for all who have struggled with life's growing pains—and lived to laugh about it. My desire is that these humorous short stories will be a departure from reality that will amuse and entertain.

I wrote this book for you to keep close at hand to remind yourself: *When life happens...laughter begins.*

I hope you will laugh along with me...or at me! That's okay, too.

XO, Lee

Lee-isms

Me—Summer 1979
(Bayfield, Wisconsin)

You Got It, Kid!

Me—all grown up

My mom has been telling me for years: "Enjoy it while you got it, kid!"

Since her recent trek through menopause and the common frustrations associated with aging, I have unavoidably glimpsed the "exciting" developments a woman must inevitably endure.

Hot flashes, the disappearance of your waistline, and loss of sex drive—simply because the vagina decided it has had enough and begins to atrophy.

2

Body parts are no longer where they are supposed to be, and as the days go by, the woman staring back in the bathroom mirror suddenly resembles a *Picasso*.

Woman sitting in an armchair
(Pablo Picasso—1920)

You are also the proud new owner of a permanent flotation device that is attached to your waistline and will never be removed no matter how much you exercise, eat right, or bitch about it. The silver lining in this is that since your brain has waned in the last fifty-some years (and you have forgotten how to swim, among other millions of things), if you were to fall overboard on one of those senior cruises, you would just float to safety.

Yet, your husband, if he is still around and hasn't traded you in for a newer model, looks better than the day you married and is randier than most eighteen-year-olds. God forbid his friend, the Doctor, gives him a prescription for *Viagra*!

Another satisfied customer

By now, you are probably asking yourself, *Why is a young woman concerned with a matter that won't affect her for years to come?*

Well, for one, I am a woman, and this is what I have to look forward to. You progress, not regress, and in a lot of ways I am thankful for that. For a slew of other reasons, I am a nervous wreck.

Women in society shoulder a lot of responsibility and expectations. Of course we are "supposed" to remain beautiful, young, and firm forever. Our worth is somehow judged by this more than anything else. Girls out of the school room have already had plastic surgeries; we are doing some maintenance work in our thirties, becoming "Botox Beauties" in our forties, and starting over from scratch in our fifties! God knows what's left after that.

Between what our body does naturally as it "matures" or falls apart, how society views us, and our own insecurities, it is no wonder so many of us have a difficult time with the aging process.

When I turned thirty, I suddenly realized that everything had changed overnight. Society in general seemed to be perversely fascinated with my single status, a topic not just discussed at family functions, but with complete strangers like the sweet senior citizen behind the register at the local market.

After scanning my "bachelorette" groceries and brown-bagging my bottle of *Pinot Noir*, she sadly shook her head. Frowning, she gave a *tsk, tsk*.

"You're not getting any younger, Cookie. You should be sharing that wine with a nice young man." Horrified, I felt like asking the well-meaning old bat to wait while I grab a razor to go with my *Pinot*.

Then, there is the shelf-life of my eggs. No one had ever informed me that as I age, my eggs do too. This seems to be another important *thirty-something* issue.

With no prospect of children in my present-to-near future, if I do decide to have babies, it will be with rotten eggs. I read somewhere that the longer I wait, the development, intelligence, agility, and basic overall health of my future children could be affected. So I'm picturing slow, stupid babies, which if I'm lucky, will make it into community college. And if I wait till forty, well, we're talking GED. I know this can't be accurate—just thoughts my mind likes to torture me with.

When I meet new people, I am no longer the youngest in the group. Nope, I'm the old one, the one that everyone gauges their success or lack thereof by: *I got plenty of time; I'll never end up like her.* See, I can also help with depression.

I admit that I enjoy it when I get carded and thank the person like I've seen my mother do. I always thought she was such a dork when I was younger and would roll my eyes and laugh as she happily handed over her identification, while beaming and giggling like a schoolgirl.

Instead of being annoyed, I readily show my I.D. and thank the little girl rolling her eyes behind the counter. *I'm only THIRTY for Christ sakes! Just you wait sweetheart, you'll be thirty someday, and someone will be rolling their pubescent eyes at you!*

But then certain things never change. When a semi-truck pulls alongside me on the interstate honking his horn, and scaring the hell out of me, I smile, and wave, and think to myself, *You got it, kid!* Instead of, *You Ass, are you trying to kill me?!*

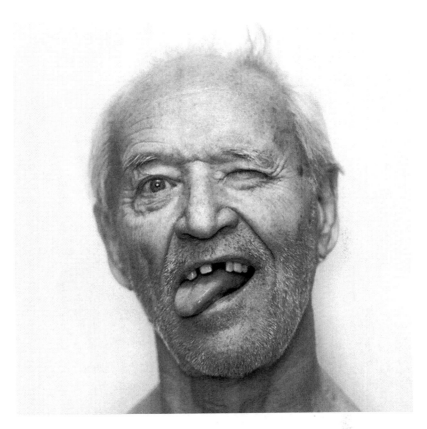

He may be one of the worst characters you've ever had panting at you, but as his eighteen-wheeler erratically merges into your lane, you have to give him credit—he is multi-tasking.

Hanging out of the window, resting his index and middle finger on each side of his mouth like a "V" while plunging his fat, slobbering tongue in and out like some starved reptile feeling for its slower-moving prey, he manages to handle his rig with his one free hand. Periodically pointing at the bumper sticker on his extended cab that says, *It's not the size of the worm, but how you wiggle it that counts!*

Yes, enjoy it, because that heinous spectacle is fleeting. The *Peterbilt* horns will stop blowing, our county's finest road construction crews will stop whistling and calling me *Mami*. And forget the days of receiving a wink and free drink. It will all soon be a thing of the past.

When I hit that stage in my life and start sagging, I hope I will grow old tastefully, and comfortable within myself, not like the women I've seen in the mall with the long blond hair and stiletto heels.

From the back she looks twenty-five, then she turns around and you're like, *Good God!* No amount of surgery is going to make a seventy-five year old woman look twenty-five, and who in their right mind would want to?

I love to watch the guys who spot her from behind. The young males with raging hormones will actually spout off something like, *Damn!*

While waiting for their wives to hurry up, the older men, with their raging hormones, are speaking even louder, but only with their eyes.

Then she turns towards him. Excitement transforms into shock and revulsion, followed by denial, ending in embarrassment. Once the poor fellow pulls himself together, his adamant expression of superiority clearly states, *I wasn't checking THAT out in the first place!*

I guess you could try and stay twenty-five forever, or you could grow old gracefully, flotation device and all. With luck, you'll have a randy, but faithful husband that loves you and wants you just the way you are. Or maybe he could just have cataracts—in both eyes!

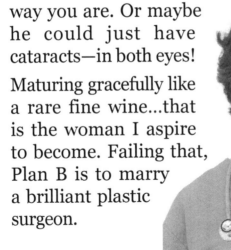

Maturing gracefully like a rare fine wine...that is the woman I aspire to become. Failing that, Plan B is to marry a brilliant plastic surgeon.

Possible future husband

I like to sleep in

and

go to bed early.

My Left Breast, My Right Thigh

Zealous and green, I sauntered into my first Children's Writers group, assembling in the back of a local book store. My heels clicked while the author who led the meeting lost his voice and watched me walk. I cannot say for sure exactly what he was gawking at, but I think it was my left breast and my right thigh. I like to call him Crazy Eyes.

You know those people who are cock-eyed, and you feel

so uncomfortable because you don't know which eye to look at, and then you wonder if they know that you don't know which eye to focus on? Suddenly, you're concerned that they might be as uncomfortable about it as you are. I found a seat, sat next to a woman, and thought, *Where is everyone?*

Considering this was to be an established group affiliated with the *Writer's Alliance*, I assumed it would have been larger than Crazy Eyes and the lady beside me. Crazy Eyes introduces himself by saying, "Have you ever seen the movie, *A Beautiful Mind*?"

Enthusiastically, I replied, "Why yes, I have."

"I am just like the guy in that movie; I hear voices." *Oh good God!*

Enriching the next twelve and half minutes of our lives, he explained how he recently saw his doctor at the VA who instructed him to never inform him about these voices again, or, as a medical professional, he would have no other choice but to admit him to a mental facility for immediate observation. Crazy Eyes graciously shared with the group how he had responded to his doctor. "But Doc, they're nice now, not like they use to be. They were incredibly vicious before. It got so bad that I had to live alone on top of a mountain. I came down only once a week for groceries because they were so sadistic and...and just plain wicked. You don't want to know what they use to tell me to do! But now they help me write and illustrate my children's stories for my picture books."

I'm not sure what his doctor had to say to that because in walked a giant of a redneck with long, salt-and-pepper hair and a scruffy beard. He appeared to be more than two hundred and sixty pounds, and probably six feet six without his alligator boots. Actually, I was more interested in his triple X big and tall T-shirt. It had only two huge, black, block letters—*FU*.

Between Crazy Eyes and FU, I thought to myself, *Am I in the right place? I am at the Children's Writers group, right?*

FU stomped up, leaving gravel in his wake, the evidence of tempestuous winds, with the smell of exhaust lingering in his tangled hair. "Is this here 'at writers' meetin'?"

"Yes it is," Crazy Eyes eagerly answered. Just one more person for him to ask if they have ever seen *A Beautiful Mind*. Somehow I doubt FU has seen that one.

FU told Crazy Eyes in his southern drawl (not the pretty Carolina kind, rather, the redneck drawl that makes each word sound like it's been bushhogged), "I jes gots ta get published! I don't know nuttin 'bout typin', don't know whut's I'm doin', I jus tell my sis, she dun all dat stuff fo me. But den she up an gots 'erself knocked up en married off. So I gots my stories, and nows I hav ta tryin' type it all up fo

13

mahself. An I jus wanna get published. I'm heres ta find out how ya go 'bout doin' dat?"

At this point, I decided to salvage what was left of this fiasco and acquaint myself with the lady sitting beside me.

A lean and leggy insignificant woman in her mid-forties, with long, untamed auburn curls, introduced herself as *Margarita-Runs-With-The-Wind*.

"You can call me Rita-Runs-With-The-Wind, for short. My mother was an alcoholic and named me after her favorite drink. We don't talk much

anymore and I have always preferred Rita—and Scotch."

Amused by her hilarity, Rita sat laughing—and snorting. She told me her last name use to be Smith, but it did not express her true nature so she legally changed it to Runs-With-The-Wind.

"Cowboy—he's my boyfriend for the moment—has been so supportive, patient, and understanding about my writing that I am going to dedicate my first book to him. He really does deserve it." She turned to face me more squarely and locked her eyes on mine before continuing.

"I'm writing from personal experiences, yah know, and I'm reliving actual events daily. Unfortunately, it has been emotionally draining and extremely taxing on our sex life. I've even had to quit my job to work full time on this!" I furrowed my brow and nodded, knowingly, with the look of sincere understanding of her sacrifice and dedication.

"My book is written specifically for mothers to read and discuss with their daughters," Rita continued. "It deals with abuse, and how to not wind up with the wrong man. Girls need to know what I know, what I've learned the hard way. You see, when you wake up in a hospital with your head bashed in, it really changes a person!"

Mouth wide open, mind spinning, I gripped the edges of the cheap plastic chair so I wouldn't fall. I felt its flexibility and texture under my slick palms.

The contact grounded me enough to quell my impulse to run out of the store's Emergency Exit. Instead, I contemplated all she had said.

As I closed my mouth and hung on tight, I asked, "We are talking about first readers, right? Children anywhere from four to seven in age?"

"Yeah, something like that. Little girls need to learn at a young age what to look for so they don't end up in an abusive relationship," Rita replied, matter-of-factly.

"Just wondering," was all I said aloud. *Mothers will be reading this book to their daughters at bedtime?—Like hell they will! Cowboy deserves his dedication.*

At this point, I decided I had had enough. (Can you blame me?!) I politely said my *good-byes*, and "yes," I would "try" to make next month's meeting.

As I left the book store, I ran into an acquaintance. As our casual conversation ended, he asked about my cat, Prozac.

I did not know it at the time, but Crazy Eyes was lurking behind me and got all excited, jumping and twitching like the oddest animated cartoon, saying, "*Prozac*, you have *Prozac*?" *Oh, for Christ sakes! As if I'm on it, and now we have something in common! We could go back to my place, share some Prozac, and if it doesn't affect our libidos, and he can focus, we could have a mutually gratifying, eye-poping, erotic encounter.* Disgusting, repulsive,

in hand (his favorite), while repeatedly *OH-ZAAC,* over and over.

Prozac at 11 years old (2009)
...only two lives remaining

...e first incident, only those dwelling in ...g 10311 spoke to me, knowing I was not ...le, just an eccentric but harmless *cat lady,* ...pstairs.

..., I was considered normal, even boring in ...rison to other Psych Ward occupants. For ...le, the fireman in apartment #309 was a  liability. He would go to work for 72 hours and leave his iron on, or stove... sometimes both! I'd get a frantic phone call at ...m. from the Forgetful Firefighter to please go ...t door and check for him.

an absolute abomination! He still reminds me of one of the monsters from the book, *Where the Wild Things Are.*

"We will call you if you give me your number." That's what Crazy Eyes said. Who's *we*? Probably all those friendly voices that help him write children's books! What are his voices saying about me? I don't want to know. My one voice is telling me, *Run. Run fast!*

He said he would be willing to work with me anytime *eye to eye. Did he seriously just say that?* Yes, he did; but it was too easy for me to state the obvious, so instead I joked, saying, "In a well-lit area, when pigs fly?" He didn't get my humor; he just stood there eyeballing my left breast and right thigh. Maybe one of his voices will explain it to him after I am far, far away.

If you don't have anything nice to say...

write it down

—you can reach more people that way.

The
At A

green olives
calling, PR(

At one time or anoth
hand knowledge of
reminds me of family,
your family, you can
The experiences have
entertaining, but I am l
home owner now, and s\

One of my last and most r
Addison Park Apartments
only where I called "home,
to by tenants as the "Psych

It was late February when
residence, and by March 2(
the rest of the Ward's inhabi

I was the peculiar girl in #30(
the night, and not clocking in
five job come morning. Ignora
was a freelance writer and reg
stories—often times about ther
stigma of total enigma given to
my case living with a black cat na
had a penchant for falling off the
failed attempts to catch a lizard,
or amphibian. Especially, when I
found tearfully traversing the neigl

After th
buildin
certifia
living u

In fact
compa
exam

4 a
nex

When he wasn't working, he was drinking. This Emergency Medical Technician no longer had screens on his upstairs bedroom windows. *Why*, you may ask. *Is it some sort of fire hazard unbeknownst to the general public?* No, he would blackout and then pass out, wake up to go to the bathroom, mistake his window for a toilet, and relieve himself onto the neighbors (dying) petunias below.

The lady downstairs, who could never figure out why her flowers wouldn't grow, was actually a celebrity in some circles. April Showers was elderly now, but back in her day, she was quite *the dish*.

From a small town in Illinois, April took off for Chicago before finishing high school. There, she became a headlining burlesque dancer under the stage name, the *Contorting Contessa*. She dated mafia men, was adored by many Chicagoans, and even became her hometown of Effingham County's *Milton Bradley* Twister Champion in 1975.

Sadly, before the end of 1977, the Contorting Contessa vanished from the Chicago nightlife scene. Some say she and Elvis Presley ran away together, since the King died around the same time. Others are convinced that the Contessa was directly involved in the FBI investigation, *Operation Family*

Secrets; she, along with a *Chicago Outfit* affiliate, were reported to be living in Miami where they were proprietors of the *Bearded Clam*, a small seafood restaurant popular with locals. However, none of that was true.

One cloudy, spring day in May, 1977, April Showers was practicing a new routine when she dislocated both her hips while visiting her sister in Boston, Massachusetts. After months of recovery and endless physical therapy, April's doctors advised that a warmer climate may be more therapeutic. She packed up and moved to Florida, where she has been living on disability and diamonds from past lovers over the last four decades.

Then there was the *Sweet Señorita* in #203 with Hepatitis C...which wasn't the only thing she had been spreading, just ask any of her Sugar Daddies.

Agreed amongst all tenants, the most fascinating occupant in the Ward was the old man upstairs from Sweet Señorita, and located directly across from me, in #303.

No one had ever met him, but we all felt as if we knew him—intimately. Thursday through Saturday, from 9 p.m. until 9:15 p.m., if you went outside or were coming home late from work, you would see him— and he would perform for you. Outfitted in a red  silk teddy and black high heels, Gramps would dance for the world at his window. Some nights he took his moves out onto his balcony, where he notoriously cooled down by showcasing his latest yoga postures he'd learned at the local YMCA—still donning six-inch heels.

Ahhh...sometimes I admit I miss the good ole days of beer-scented petunias and Dancing Queens. Moving to a quiet cul-de-sac on a golf course, I gave up the entertaining distractions and authentic characters of the Psych Ward. Inevitably, my new neighborhood would get a healthy sampling of unorthodox happenings that only a former Psych Ward resident, with a carry-over penchant for livening things up, could manage.

I ultimately adopted a pig from Texas—which totally proves my point. Now, I could have named him "Bacon"; golfers would have thought I had a protein deficiency when calling his name. After all, I have matured, and so instead I named him "Officer." Officer Volpe...and I am finally getting the respect I deserve!

Me with Officer the Mini Pig (2015)

I'm An 80 Percenter!

Yesterday:

I bought an advertisement to promote LeeVolpe. com. I put in a short description of my website, added a profile picture, set the age range and category of interests, and voilà! I can't tell you how excited I was—yesterday.

Today:

I logged in to check the results of my online promotion and saw I had one new fan. *Not bad,* I thought, and decided to investigate. Clicking on *Website Ad Results,* I found my announcement had reached over 8,000 people in less than 24 hours, but had only three views, and as we already know, only one *nethead* signed up. The kicker is that I received a notice advising me that I am at an "80% negativity rate" and to insure future success, I should "revise" my blurb.

So basically what they are telling me is 80% of viewers decided they didn't like me in less than 24 hours, and I paid them to do it. Am I the only one that finds this hilarious?!

Obviously, I will edit my web endorsement, and I will keep you posted on my percentages, but I have to look at it this way:

Yesterday, 80% of people didn't even know who I was, but today they do.

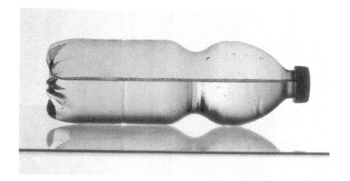

"May you always view the glass half-full."
—Lee Volpe

"You're a Lefty!"

"No," I answered, "I am a writer."

Give Me Your Tired, Your Poor...Your Blind, Your Hispanophones

I never considered the visually disabled when designing my logo.

I am specifically referring to a commonly inherited, predominantly male handicap known as *color blindness*. It only recently occurred to me when my logo, which contains the letters of my name, received a comment on my website.

One reader wrote, "All I see are the letters spelling 'LOVE PEOPLE'. I dig!"

My viewer was male—and color blind. Most likely suffering from red-green color blindness.

Having an Italian father who was impaired with this very condition, though he'd never admit it (or the fact he was only 5 feet, 6 inches), prepared me to navigate this familiar terrain.

Unfortunately, someone with this kind of visual deficiency would confuse red with yellow and beige, which are the colors I chose for my logo—therefore, they could never see my name, *Lee Volpe*, at all.

Ironically, my website is becoming very popular in Mexico—where no one speaks English! I have no clue what the comments say. So, now I finally have an English-speaking fan commenting, and he can't see shit!

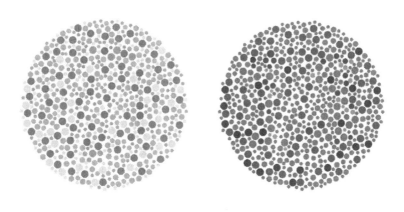

Ishihara Color Blindness Test
(If you're only seeing this in black and white—well, duh...)

The Admission Letter

I was so excited the day my letter from the Admissions Office arrived. I desperately wanted to go to the University of South Florida. The best school in the country for my education and career interests? No. My boyfriend was already a member of the student

body, and most of my friends were heading there in the fall...as I hoped for myself.

I held my breath as I slowly opened the envelope and unfolded the letter.

Dear Lee,

Congratulations! It is with great pleasure that I offer you admission to the University of South Florida Class of 1998...

I was IN! I was so excited! I couldn't wait to tell everyone, which didn't take long. Proud family, excited boyfriend and long-time friends I could finally make future plans with. I was so happy.

Calling to set up my campus tour, I contacted Admissions for information. And then it happened—

of course it would happen to me, and I doubt anyone can say it has happened to them.

What, pray tell, happened?

"We are sorry to inform you, Miss Volpe, but there seems to have been an unfortunate error and we will not be welcoming you to our university this semester. You're not on our *approved* enrollment list for fall students," the woman on the phone awkwardly informed me.

"But I have a document confirming my acceptance and it is formally signed by the head of Admissions!" I frantically countered.

Sadly, incredibly, the woman was right. A mistake had been made, and I had NOT been accepted to the University of South Florida. I now had to somehow inform the world. What the hell was I supposed to say: *Just kidding! Psych!*

Thankfully, the University of Tampa offered me a grant to attend their school. It was a private college with an excellent academia. How I got in, I'll never know; maybe they needed to pad the  roster demographics with SWFs (Shunned White Freshmen) that semester.

Nevertheless, it provided me with the perfect explanation to inform the world why I would not be a *Bull*, but a *Spartan* instead.

Today, as high-schoolers are receiving college acceptance or rejection letters, I wonder how many are incorrectly informed, how many change schools at the last minute, and how many will look back and realize they ended up exactly where they were supposed to be?

Bulls suck; Go Spartans!

Being a writer is the greatest revenge.

Not only can you "write" wrongs,

but you also get the last WORD!

Freeballing

A business acquaintance called the other day to share her Monday with me. We have become fast friends and she's a fan of my humor—which doesn't hurt.

She informed me that every Monday morning she takes an *aqua yoga* class at her local YMCA. On this particular Monday she had a mid-morning meeting scheduled at her office downtown.

Prepared, she headed to her health club wearing a swim suit and cover-up, while bringing all the essentials to get showered and changed afterwards.

All was going smoothly, until she started to get dressed and couldn't locate her panties. *Freeballing* was not an option in her Diane von Fürstenberg wrap dress, while meeting with new clients. Panic began...and then she thought: *What would Lee do? ...Lee would laugh!*

So my friend chuckled and finished getting ready. Ironically, as she gathered up her belongings, attached to the hanger was a pair of *no show* underwear.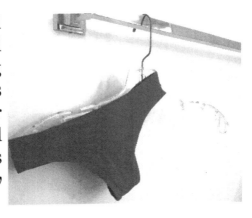

<u>Moral of the story:</u> *When there is nothing left to do, just LAUGH!*

(Also, my friend will soon learn—first I *laugh*, and then I *write*. You never know what could end up in a book!)

Lee Volpe—where laughter begins

Forty Is the New Eighty

You're forty?! The young, blonde, fitness model at the gym responded with blunt astonishment.

"Yes, I am very forty! I get up early, I listen to talk radio, I found a gray hair, I need readers, and my dermatologist just confirmed my very first age spot from sun damage. You don't get any more forty than that!"

"I have a friend who has a crush on you," Barbie said. "I didn't realize your age when I showed him your picture; but I don't think he'll mind you being old."

A half an hour later, this youthful, ideal specimen of the female form had not only called me "elderly," but overweight and lazy. Recovering from two broken ankles and under doctor's orders to stay off my feet, garnered no compassion nor understanding from Workout Barbie.

I was visiting with one of my dearest friends when I shared what had happened to me at the gym.

'You're forty?" His response was laced with disbelief, and something else; was it disappointment? "I guess I didn't realize..." he quietly mumbled, "...you are officially out of my dating bracket," was his official verdict.

That Sunday evening, I met a friend and her boyfriend at a favorite spot on the water for watching the sunset and listening to local live music. As my friend was dancing, a bald black man in his early sixties, and approximately 6 feet, 7 inches, joined her on the dance floor. I turned to her boyfriend on my left and asked, "Who's the guy?"

"Just an old friend from around town," he told me.

As I watched the man awkwardly dance, and miss every other beat, I realized he had absolutely no rhythm.

"He may be the only black man I have ever seen who can't dance," I observed aloud.

"We call him *Spastic Colon*," the boyfriend offhandedly added.

As the next song began and our two dancers were warmed up and glistening with perspiration,

I wondered what other contradictions lay within this anomaly they called, *Spastic Colon*.

"I bet he has a small penis," I speculated.

With no comments on my verbal assumptions, I continued rambling. "99% of black men have big penises and can dance. He has to be the 1%," I said conclusively regarding my simulated calculations.

"What are you talking about, Lee, he's not black," my friend's boyfriend declared.

As I lowered my sunglasses and squinted through the light of the setting sun, I momentarily glimpsed Spastic Colon, and immediately recognized him to be of the Caucasian race—which explained everything...EXCEPT how I thought this tall, old, white guy was a tall, bald, black one, who couldn't dance, and was lacking in the inseam.

As the evening progressed and the crowd continued to marinate, my friend's boyfriend got a little louder than his normal New York Italian self. There was a senior couple at the table in front of us, and every time we got too noisy, the husband would turn abruptly to stare in our direction, shaking his head in disapproval. I didn't understand why he was so annoyed until the band played their last song of the evening. The husband put his arm around his wife, and swayed to the music; when he looked into her twinkling eyes, he again shook his head...because he had *Parkinson's!*

Steve Aoki

Twenty minutes later when we got up to leave, I recognized the image on the young man's shirt walking beside us toward the parking lot. It was the face of Steve Aoki, the famous DJ. One of Aoki's logos is a negative space outlined likeness of his face, hair, and beard.

As we passed the guy, I commented, "Cool shirt. I love Steve Aoki!"

"I know Steve and he's cool, but this isn't him. It's *Jesus,*" he flatly announced.

Jesus Christ!

After I found *Jesus,* I decided it was time to call it a day. I phoned my mom as I was driving home and shared my Sunday Fun-day adventures with her. After updating her on the news that I was old, fat, and lazy, not to mention, blind and currently *born-again,* I began

Jesus Christ!

complaining about the permanent damage to my ankles and feet I sustained from my fall the year before.

After completing my bitch session, my mother—sensitive to my pain and desperately wanting to "fix it," concluded that she probably should have aborted me forty years ago.

Four decades later, and she's thinking abortion is the most useful solution to my declining youth; that is her rationale?!

To be fair, she was sleep-deprived and trying to be the ever-so-helpful problem-solver. Mind you, this is the same woman who posted a picture of my red-haired niece on my birthday thinking it was me!

My mother doesn't even recognize who came out of her own vagina, and she's only had two children—not sure about abortions.

In my reflections of my Sunday, I realize I have learned many things. However, most importantly, I have decided that forty may be *over the hill*, but I'd rather be over it, then under it.

A writer will never stop writing.

Only when there are no words left

will the story end.

Black Sheep Tries Bleach

Every Fourth of July, Christmas, and sometimes Thanksgiving, I spend with family—grandparents, brothers, sisters, cousins, and all their  children. I'm the baby—at 40 years old, and I am still at the kids' table.

I'm not certain whether it is the fact that I am single, having never married, with no offspring and happily living with a farm animal, or that I chose a "hobby" for my profession, but I have grudgingly come to accept my place as the *Black Sheep.*

Let's face it; it's easier to pick on the little guy, the "party of one" standing alone, defenseless, on the far edge of the herd with no protector by their side. As a scapegoat and black sheep, it's no wonder I love hoofed animals and have a mini pig for a son.

What started as an occasional way for my family members to relate to me soon became part of the Family Creed. Right in the Mission Statement, it must have stated that, "The role of the Black Sheep will be fulfilled by Lee. Everyone must comply with the Standard Operating Procedures, starting with never forgetting the fact that she is different from the rest of us."

I faded into the background so someone else could have the spotlight. I put other's feelings, wants, and needs before my own. I have loved unconditionally, defended loyally, and accepted ALL without judgment or offense. This Black Sheep tried bleach— and it didn't work.

I am stubborn. I never stop fighting, and so that's what I decided to do. I became a writer in hopes I would be heard. Yet, no one in my family reads my work; they find it to be an "acquired" taste that most people wouldn't find humorous. I backed myself into a corner and never saw "the light" again. Patrick

Me, being...well, me!

Swayze is unfortunately dead, so no one showed up to explain that, "Nobody puts Baby in the corner."

Now please understand I love my family; they are the most important thing to me, maybe because I have yet to have my own. Nevertheless, they are *my* people—some of whom I wouldn't have chosen, but we all know how that goes.

I have come to the realization that sometimes those who know us best, know us least, and may take us for granted; whereas, acquaintances may see us clearly and actually appreciate us for who we really are. Still, what is most important is how you see yourself. I find different things to remind me of who I am, rather than who others tell me I am.

You may be saying to yourself: *This story isn't so funny; where's the humor?*

Well folks, *life* isn't always funny. You have to FIND the humor, create your own laughter, and never forget your authentic self.

Let me introduce myself: My name is Lee, the little sister, the youngest daughter, the Black Sheep of my family.

Me and Pepper, the black sheep of Miss Margie's Farm
(Eagle River, WI)

#FML

"I am having an allergic reaction to my life."—Lee Volpe

#FML Moment 24

Running late for church, you trip and fall down the center aisle yelling, "Jesus Christ!"

Dress above your head, bottom up and bared, as the entire congregation focuses in on the sparkling angel wing logo of your pink lace panties.

You stand tall, finishing with, "...is the son of God. Amen."

FML

#FML Moment 47

When you return home from vacation and your *smart* scale reads, "Unknown User."

So, you check the *Help* section of the user guide which states: "You may have gained weight and your *smart* scale no longer recognizes you."

FML

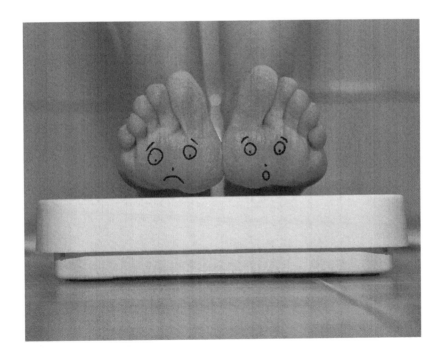

#FML Moment 10

I had been having continuous construction at my house and the final step was the painting process. The painter showed up, assistant in tow, and began applying my chosen color samples to the wall.

I'm friendly (too friendly, I have been told), which gets me in trouble most of the time; therefore, the painter was obviously feeling comfortable with my accommodating attitude.

While his partner continued working, he began telling me his life story, concentrating on his recent release from prison, finding Jesus, and the *Church of What's Happenin' Now.*

Fifteen minutes later, his assistant finished and it was time for me to make my final decision. Happy our conversation was almost at a close, I asked the painter his professional opinion of the two colors on the left.

He told me he was color blind and consulted with his partner instead. The assistant looked, and finally replied, "I'm blind in my left eye and can only make out the two colors on the right."

FML

#FML Moment 89

When I said, "Drop me anywhere," this is NOT what I intended.

Really?!

FML

I am convinced this donation bin originally accepted SHOES.

#FML Moment 101

I was on social media the other day when I saw an advertisement for a new site: *Find your twin stranger or facial look-alike.*

Intrigued, I signed up, uploaded the required images, and my search began.

It didn't take long for me to realize my self-esteem was going to suffer before my *twin* was found. I even entered my gender as *female*, not that that helped!

My doppelgänger was an overweight Asian BOY!

FML

#FML Moment 122

That moment you realize you are now the adult in the family!

FML

Mommy being silly at the supermarket

#FML Moment 22

Flirting, you become so flustered when you're saying *goodbye*, you slam your car door...WITH YOUR HEAD IN IT!

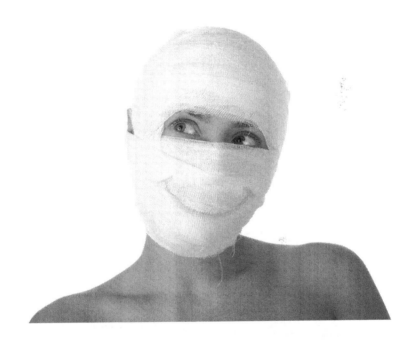

When the poor guy asks if you are all right, you reply, "Oh, I'm fine. It happens all the time."

Really? REALLY!

FML

#FML Moment 61

When your friend "tells it like it is" regarding your choice of flattering outfits:

Friend: *Do you have a longer shirt?*

Me: *I'm wearing a tunic!*

Friend: *Maybe darker pants would be more slimming?*

Me: *They're BLACK; it doesn't get any darker!*

FML

#FML Moment 9

When I was in my early twenties, I entered an essay in an online writing contest. The winner would be published in an anthology of short stories and receive a check for one hundred dollars.

It appeared legit and I was trying desperately to get my work noticed; this seemed like a logical next step towards my goal.

One month later, I received a letter congratulating me on being one of the five finalists!

My mother was with me when I got the news, and while we screamed and cried out with excitement, I continued reading. Last year's winner was listed at the bottom of the letter—with a picture.

WTF?! I groaned.

Last year's recipient was a five-year-old girl, named Madison, who wrote a poem about her guinea pig, *Sprinkles.*

FML

#FML Moment 40

Once people find out I am a *humor writer,* they have a lot to say...and a lot they shouldn't.

Here are my *Top 3* things one should never utter:

#1. "Say something funny."

You would assume I am a trained dog that can do tricks on command.

Well, folks, this *bitch* only plays dead.

#2. "You should write my life story; I'm funny as hell!"

Excuse me, but have you read anything I've written? I'm not exactly lacking in material.

And finally...

#3. "My friend so-and-so is the funniest person I know."

Say what? You know ME!

FML

#FML Moment 13

Today was the day—the first day of the rest of my life. This was the opportunity I had been working for, and today would be the first step towards fulfilling my life goals.

As I walked into the national public relations office of a highly recognized and respected publicist, I looked to my publisher, who had been an instrumental part of this whole process, for reassurance as we entered the boardroom.

They had done their homework and already had the home page of my website displayed on a giant monitor in front of the room. However, I immediately found out that my site did not represent me or my sense of humor.

"Do you want my honest option?" the celebrity publicist asked.

"Yes, please. I would appreciate any and all feedback," I genuinely replied.

"Well, I was initially excited when I saw you were a humor writer, so I checked out your webpage. I clicked on the tab called, *For a Good Time*, and..."

Yes, and? I held my breath; this was it!

"...And frankly, I didn't have a good time," she finished.

FML

Postscript: We did have a fun, successful meeting, and are currently working together.

I guess I'm better in person...

and will have to create a more comparable social media persona.

The Lineage of Lee: It's Hereditary!

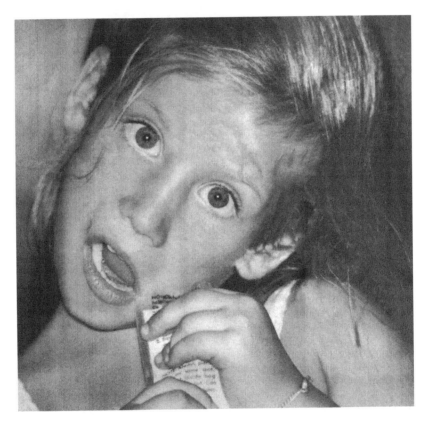

Me (5 years old)

The Amazing Adventures of Amah

Have you ever met a writer who *fucks up* the story? Well, let me introduce myself.

From childhood, my imagination has been wild—like, in first grade when my teacher got pregnant, and I asked my parents where babies came from. My basic understanding was that two people fell in love, got married, and did "adult" things— like golf.

Amah—photographer's assistant and model (Chicago 1942-1944)

So, when I raised my hand in class to share this information, my translation of events went something like this:

"Daddy has to play with his balls all by himself, because Mommy doesn't like golf." And then, "I'm gonna make sure my husband doesn't like basketball, because I want children."

I would somehow interpret and then remember events much, much differently from the reality in which they were born. My maternal grandmother, whom we called *Amah*, seemed to be the source for much of my confusion.

For example: In Third Grade we were learning about *Crazy Horse*, the leader of the Lakota (Sioux). I was much more informed on this topic than the other children hearing it for the first time. You see, Amah knew Korczak Ziolkowski, the artist who sculpted the Crazy Horse Memorial in the Black Hills of South Dakota. She was invited to his daughter's wedding who had married the son of one of Amah's closest friends.

So, when I raised my hand in class to share this information, my translation of events went something like this: "My Amah is best friends with Crazy Horse and was at his wedding!"

Example Two: In Fifth Grade we were learning about the great tales of Edgar Allan Poe— another figure I was familiar with. Amah had told me, long before, that when she was at boarding school she used to read his stories before bed and they scared her so much she'd have nightmares.

Amah at Korczak Ziolkowski's daughter's wedding reception (Black Hills, SD)

So, when I raised my hand in class to share this information, my translation of events went something like this: "My grandmother dated Edgar Allan Poe when she was young, and he scared her. He was a bad boyfriend, but she liked his bird."

Amah—photographer's assistant and model (Chicago 1942-1944)

Example Three: I started off as a film major in college. During one class, we were analyzing the movie, *The Wizard of Oz*—a favorite of mine. As you've probably guessed, I had some "inside" information unbeknownst to the rest of the group about Margaret Hamilton, the original actress to play the *Wicked Witch of the West*. Amah knew someone in the congregation at Hamilton's hometown church and she told Amah that Margaret had actually been a teacher before her acting career, and really loved children. I still believe that Amah revealed this information so I would no longer be scared of the mean and terrifying green witch...and it worked!

So, when I raised my hand in class to share this information, my translation of events went something like this: "The Wicked Witch of the West

was my grandmother's Sunday school teacher—
honest to God!"

My name is Lee Volpe; *I fuck up stories.*

Amah and me (Summer 1986)

Jacaranda Boulevard

A wonderland of Jacaranda trees in full bloom

"Are you belted in? What about you back there?"

"YES, MOMMY!" I leaned forward, eyes closed tight, and shouted from my belly's bottom, just as she was putting the car in reverse and had turned to look over her right shoulder before backing up.

Eager to be on our way and not yet having mastered "volume control" at six, I then had my mother calmly inform me there was no need to yell, especially when I was sitting directly behind her; it was not safe to do when someone was driving. "When you yell like that you scare Mommy—it is very dangerous to frighten the driver because Mommy could crash. Besides, you are going to make me deaf!"

Trying to see something, anything, out the window besides the blue, cloudless sky of the Sunshine State was occupying all of my attention. I thought there might be a doggie looking out the window of a passing car, but I was too short to peek. The seat belt was uncomfortable; I couldn't even lay down with my *blue blankie* and take a nap. However, my mother's hearing was a priority, so when she asked me if I was listening, if I understood, I whispered so low I should have used sign language so she could comprehend.

"AAAAAAHHHHHHH!" The front right-seat passenger gave a shrill, startled cry, while pointing out the window and grabbing her chest as if having a heart attack, interrupting the front seat-back seat nonverbal exchange of my mom's very cool, *I'm running out of patience,* expression as she eyed me in the rearview mirror.

With mom's composure already strained by her backseat passenger, she refocused her attention. Alarmed, she hollered, "WHAT?"

I prepared to crash.

My great, great Aunt Ida took a deep, shaky breath, and cried, "PURPLE!" She was pointing at the blossoming Jacaranda whose petals glistened in the sun, all the while littering the earth beneath its roaming branches. As I gazed at those loitering blooms, I found it magical. They made me happy, like they had made Aunt Ida.

I gave a hoot, and a boisterous "Oooooooohhhhh," dramatically dragging it out towards the end just to make sure all within hearing would have no doubts about how I was feeling.

My great, great Aunt Ida was just as tall as I was, thanks to her small frame, arthritis, and an advanced case of osteoporosis. No wonder she got so excited—we could both finally see something!

Once my poor mother's below-normal blood pressure (which had momentarily sky-rocketed) came back down, she relaxed and enjoyed it as well.

Though I've grown and can see more out my window these days, I have always remembered that Saturday afternoon drive and what it was really about—love. A mother's love for her family, a child's love of a world barely glimpsed beyond her backseat window, and an old lady's love of scenic routes in spring.

The magnificent Jacarandas were in full bloom and Aunt Ida loved purple: purple dresses, purple parasols, and purple flowers on trees with their resting decorative petals a carpet beneath. She also loved my mother. And when she turned around as best she could to ask me if I had seen the purple trees, I completely forgot myself, exclaiming loudly, "YES, I DID! I SAW THEM!" Aunt Ida's eyes twinkled, and she smiled in utter understanding as I lowered my voice and confided, "Purple's my favorite color."

Great, great Aunt Ida and her purple parasol

*My mother always said,
"pooberty," not puberty.*

*I've often wondered how she got through
it when she could not even pronounce it.*

*My mother always said,
"...never put anything in writing,"*

so I became a writer.

*My father always said,
"Listen to your mother!"*

The Queen of Mathematics

Daddy and me (1986)

Growing up, I could bartend, tell a dirty joke, and curse in a foreign language—all before I could tell time.

By the end of Third Grade, the entire class had conquered the clock—except me. My mom, determined to not let me fall behind, spent countless hours in our kitchen using every trick to teach me to read time. She downgraded my digital watch to an analog one, which I hated. She drew a circle and cut hands out of construction paper in my favorite colors (blue and purple). Yet, it wasn't until she introduced me to the *teddy bear clock* that I was intrigued and engaged enough to learn.

Around eight on a school night—the dishes done, my father thoroughly engrossed in the latest episode of *Cheers* on the boob tube, my sister in her bedroom planning Barbie and Ken's roller skating wedding— my mom and I began to tackle *time*.

By 11:45 p.m., I finally grasped the concept, but it wasn't until an hour later that the teddy bear succeeded and I mastered telling time.

Math was another struggle for me. By the start of Sixth Grade, my mother avoided the subject entirely, deciding instead to let my father handle that department.

My parents had completely opposite teaching styles. My mom would sit patiently for hours, encouraging, finding a creative angle to use to explore, explain, and enlighten me. My father, on the other hand, would become frustrated and impatient, take over, and end up doing my homework himself.

Daddy (Summer 1986)

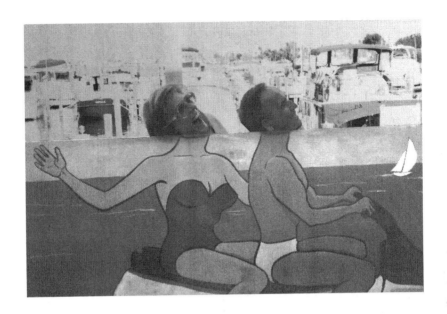

Mommy and Daddy (Fishermen's Village—Florida)

I preferred dad's help. He and I turned a deaf ear to my mother insistently pointing out that, *I wasn't learning anything!*

But it wasn't long before Daddy's help was more trouble than it was worth.

You see, my dad was failing Sixth Grade Math. Exasperated and completely dumbfounded, he concluded that my teacher's numbers had to be wrong—all the while bent on completing the next assignment.

Mommy finally came to the rescue, and after a few filthy French words from me, a whole slew of naughty Italian from my father, and enough *J & B* and water for my mother's (our teacher's) frazzled nerves, my father and I passed Sixth Grade Math.

My difficulty with numbers is still prevalent today. Don't ask me how much per-unit cost savings I get by buying the larger package. Don't ask me how old John Lennon was when he died even if you tell me the years of his birth and death. The anxiety I suffer from figuring gratuity is enough to ensure I never leave home without my laminated tip card.

I've done research and concluded that I most likely have the math disorder, *Dyscalcula*. It can be inherited from one or both parents, or can occur if your mother drank blended scotch whiskey during pregnancy.

...and my mother said,

"Karma's a bitch!"

My stepfather answered,

"Who's Karma?"

Batman's Pooper Scooper

My sister was young when she met her first husband, and married by twenty-two. Her name (Rade) rhymes with "body" and the nickname "Rade the Body" fit her to a tee. Though she did not use her "assets" the way most boys hoped, she carried the stigma as if she did. Unfortunately, when she met a nice, young man who treated her like a lady, she immediately fell "in love."

His last name was *Batman*. He was not the best-looking, nor the most masculine; between you and me, he was a horse's ass. Yet he loved my sister, treated her nice, and...I didn't have to live with him.

A year later, my sister was *Mrs. Horse's Ass Batman*, and two years after that, *and family*, was tacked on. Now, I believe my niece and nephew are the greatest creations on this green earth, besides indoor plumbing and *Google*. However, if you come from a close family like ours, then you really should think twice (or three times!) about whom you bring in to it.

While I was "pooper-scoopin'" after my mini pig Officer's breakfast at our summer home in northern Wisconsin, I wondered where this handy device had come from. Then I found out that it used to be Batman's. My sister, now divorced from the BatHole and happily remarried to the lovable Gooch Heiman (don't get me started), now admits her ex-husband was always an ass.

As I continued shoveling, I concluded that if we first thought of our family before we made commitments with others, maybe it would save us all from standing knee-deep in crap.

If you gave nary a thought before hooking up with an annoying mate, just watch and pay attention and you will notice what you are putting your loved ones through. Your poor grandfather has to listen to endless bullshit at family get-togethers, your mother picks up every check on outings because he's a user, and he talks down to your younger sister, treating her like she's ten—until he sneaks up from behind to look down her pants!

Remember, you get to go home alone with this winner, to the BatCave, and if you think he's obnoxious now, give it a minute—or twenty years!

Should there be any red flags, or *bat signals*, then I suggest that when your own version of a horse's ass asks, "Will you marry me?" you turn to them and say, "I'm busy shoveling pig shit that day."

In the end you must follow your heart and listen to your own voice. In that path lies your journey, and wisdom. Rocky roads often lead to beautiful destinations, just try not to "step in it" along the way.

Besides, there is always a bright side. In this story, the younger sister got a pooper-scooper out of the divorce!

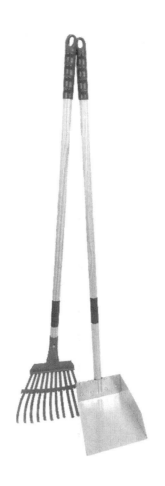

WENIS

In the backseat of my car today, my 14-year-old niece and 12-year-old nephew we're annoying each other, when my nephew informed me:

"Wendi is pulling my wenis!"

Word of the Day:
the *wenis* is the extra skin on the elbow.

Thank God!

RAH-DEE

My sister was born in the spring of 1974 to my Italian father and German mother. My maternal grandmother (Amah) was concerned that the baby would be "dark-skinned" due to my father's ethnicity. So when my sister was born, my dad delighted in the introduction of

Rade—my big sister

his mother-in-law (and best friend) to his newborn daughter.

Looking through the window of the hospital nursery at all the babies, my father pointed for my grandmother to see my sister, and said, "That one."

Amah just about fell over trying to absorb the image of the little negro baby my father was pointing at as he proclaimed, "Isn't she beautiful?!"

My dad nodded to the nursery attendant as my grandmother braced herself for the meeting of her first and very "Italian" grandchild.

The nurse reached down into a crib next to the cooing black baby boy and lifted a long-legged, fair-skinned girl, with a full head of strawberry blonde hair, and the last name, *Volpe*, on the side of her cradle. To Amah's relief, it was my sister, and they named her Rade.

Rade [RAH-DEE] was my great-grandmother's maiden name, and would now be my sister's life-long pronunciation problem and pseudonym pastime for all to play.

Rade (1974)

Commonly called Raid, or Rade Potty (when she refers to me as *Lee-Pee)*, the nickname most often used wasn't even created until she hit puberty; that is when *Rade the Body* was born. But before *The Body* nickname was conceived, I was—two-and-a-half years later, to be exact. Then her title became Big Sister.

Rade (kindergarten yearbook photo)

I looked up to her, and not just because she has always been taller, getting the nice legs in the family. Rade was my very first friend, my only friend, my best friend.

The Volpe sisters' sleepover— Rade (age 5) and me (age 3)

If I was scared in the middle of the night, I'd go to Rade's room down the hall. Sometimes she would let me sleep with her, since it was usually her stories that scared me in the first place. Other times, I just slept outside her room where her green carpet abruptly ended and the tan flooring of the hall began.

One time she allowed me to join her and her friends to watch *Children of the Corn* (a Stephen King horror flick) during her Saturday night slumber party. Over breakfast the next morning, my parents hard at work outside in the garden, Rade informed me of their plans for planting a corn field, and started humming the theme song from the movie. It took me a long time to trust that my parents were not actually growing a crop of corn in our backyard in Saint Petersburg, Florida. It also took me a long time to believe that I WASN'T adopted.

When I was four years old, my sister got mad at me and told me to pack my bags. She revealed the details of my adoption, said I wasn't living up to her expectations as a little sister, and so she was returning me. She actually pretended to call the agency to come pick me up.

As I tearfully packed my suitcase, my mom entered the room, and asked what was going on.

"I don't want to go!" I sobbed.

"RADE!" my mother yelled.

"It's okay, Mom. I told her the truth," Rade said, oh, so innocently.

Rade was born with a disability; she never developed that thing we call a *filter* or the *tact* that goes along with it. Growing up as Rade Volpe's little sister provided me with the "thick skin" I confidently wear today.

Was she a typical "older sibling," or was my torment unconventional? When Rade would get low in her piggy bank, she would come to my room. Quietly,

Rade and me (1979)

on tip-toes, in the dark of night. Now, I can sleep through anything and I have done so—fire alarms, my sister's morning cries to *wake up or we'll be late for school*, even my dad stepping on my head one night in the hall outside Rade's door. (It didn't wake me, but it almost killed my dad who thought he had broken my neck!)

I was the kid that let my baby teeth stay in as long as possible, hopefully until they fell out on their own. My sister was braver and pulled her teeth out before they were ready because she wanted money from the Tooth Fairy. Once she was out of barely loose teeth, she headed to my room in the middle of the night. I'd wake up with her wiggling my teeth, and telling me to go back to sleep. Entrepreneurial, or demented?

One time our parents repainted each of our bedrooms. Rade decided to write all over her freshly painted walls...and then blame me. It was the first and only spanking I ever got, and no matter how I professed my innocence, it fell on deaf ears. Rade was probably six years old when that happened, and it took her twenty-four more to confess her crime. On her thirtieth birthday, she finally admitted the truth—and laughed, and laughed, and laughed.

I was my sister's very first source of amusement. (Rade and me—1977)

You never knew what Rade was going to say or do next, which must have been an adventure for our parents. At four years old, she went for her annual visit to our pediatrician, Dr. Green, and during the exam Rade announced to both the doctor and my mother that something smelled.

"Mommy, Mommy, do you smell that?" Rade loudly asked. "Mommy, MOMMY, it smells really bad!" My mother desperately tried to ignore her...and the smell.

"MOMMY, MOMMY...did you pass gas?"

"No, Rade, I didn't; now sit down so Dr. Green can finish."

"Dr. Green?" My sister looked at him suspiciously. "Did you pass gas?"

When Dr. Green failed to acknowledge her, Rade got up, walked over to the door, and began opening and closing it. As she fanned out the smelly room, she waved her other hand in front of her face, dramatically displaying her disgust, while saying "*PEE-YEW*" over and over again.

I am sure most of you are curious, as was my father, whose first reaction upon hearing the story was to ask my mom, "Well, did you pass gas?"

"No!" my mother cried. "It must have been Dr. Green," she hypothesized.

When Rade was in high school and fully developed, the boys called her, Rade the Body, with good reason. Gorgeous legs for days, 34D, and NO hips and thighs! Did I mention that she also had a beautiful, younger sister, with a good personality? Well, I didn't have my sister's physique, and my sister didn't have the communication skills to deal with her overweight and sensitive littler sister.

Rade would try to help me feel more secure. One time, she pointed to an extremely obese woman on a scooter

Playing dress-up...as our parents.
I guess I was supposed
to be our father.
(Rade and me—Summer 1983)

and said, "Now THAT'S fat! Don't get me wrong, you're not skinny by any means, but at least you don't need a scooter—yet." Her consoling words made me only want to slit one wrist, instead of both.

I wasn't the only lucky recipient of Rade's wonderful compliments and words of wisdom. We had a family friend who was graduating and proudly presenting her senior picture to us. In the shot, she was leaning against a tree, with the sunlight shining through the branches, casting an amber hue on her normally brunette locks. Rade was insisting she looked like someone famous, but couldn't place it.

"You look so familiar, like a celebrity or someone I know," Rade mumbled, the wheels of her brain working and searching, until...

"I got it! You look just like the guy from the movie, *Mask*," she happily announced.

Oh my God, my sister just compared our friend to Eric Stoltz's character in the movie who had a massive facial skull deformity!

Our friend's look of horror initiated the realization of what she had just said, so to make it better, Rade finished with, "...not when he died, but earlier in the movie. Remember when he was outside and liked the sun shining on his face? Well, that's how you look with the sunlight on yours." She finished proudly, satisfied with her observation and skillful delivery.

Rade is smart, yet somehow so oblivious; decent and moral, yet sometimes a societal anomaly. She is loud in a library, cried at the end of the movie *Clueless*, and laughs if someone gets hurt—like falling down a flight of stairs. Don't misunderstand, she will offer a helping hand, but only after fully documenting the event with her camera phone, while laughing her ass off.

In college, I rescued a cat that unfortunately died at home a few weeks later. I was hysterical and couldn't deal with his lifeless body, so I called Rade.

She showed up (a little "flavored" from an evening with the girls at the local ale house) to help me dispose of my four-legged friend. Amid giggles, uncomforting comments, and observations from my inebriated sister, we somehow got through the ordeal that I would never have been able get through without her. Her ability to be inappropriate, yet amusing and helpful, is what makes her not only a rarity and complexity, but invaluable to me.

Today, Rade is still unapologetically honest and a hell of a lot of fun, but where she has acquired more aplomb, I have less.

"Little" sisters dressed up and celebrating Independence Day (July 2010)

She has learned to filter, where I have holes that words uncontrollably slip out of. She is still my long-legged partner in crime, my oldest friend, and greatest critic. Whether you call her *Raid*, *Rade Potty*, or *Rade the Body*, to *Lee Pee*, she will always be *Big Sister*.

Rade and me as adults (Christmas 2015)

Mom Behind the Wheel, Multitasking

My mother is very good at multitasking. As we drive from Wisconsin to Florida, with a Portuguese Water Dog, a cat on Prozac, and a 70-pound mini pig with an oral fixation, I grab the *Oh Shit* handle as she veers into the right lane.

"Are you all right?" I asked. "Do you need me to drive? I don't feel like dying today."

"I'm not going to kill you," she calmly said. "I just need to close my eyes for a couple minutes."

Potty Talk

Typically, I don't find "toilet humor" amusing; I prefer witty, dry, self-deprecating banter. However, I can admit that some of life's baser bodily functions, in the right context, can be entertaining. The following stories are some of those times.

Daddy (1988)

My father was on his customary weekend excursion to the hardware store, off to prowl the isles for his next home improvement project, when all of a sudden he had to *pass gas*. Looking left, then right, making sure no one was in sight, he was free to flatulate. And so he did.

A little person, who happened to be a *Lowes* employee (pun intended), walked out from behind my father. Waving his hand in front of his nose to somehow circulate fresh air into his lungs, the shrimp was steaming. Revolted, he headed as far away from my dad, and my father's uncontrollable laughter—and gas, as he could get.

My maternal grandmother, Amah, knew a woman who would stand on top of public toilet seats rather than putting paper down or squatting. Well, that was until the lady fell in the toilet at the local *Fuddruckers* and broke her ankle.

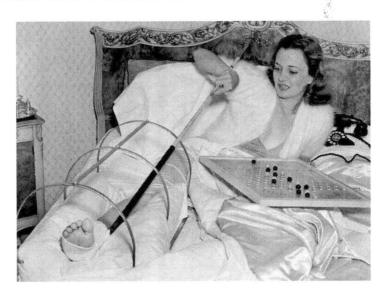

Then there was the time I stayed a month at a Residence Inn in Rochester, Minnesota, while doing some training at the Mayo Clinic. I got to know the staff and other guests rather quickly.

I remember regularly hanging out with the nightshift crew and hearing all the day's gossip. There was the wealthy eccentric socialite staying in Room 606—she was in her early forties, some relation to, "restaurant royalty," who just happened to have a very particular and bizarre habit.

While the guest in Room 606 was seeking unknown care at the clinic, the maids continually braved the daily treatment to which they were subjected. The debutante had a penchant for pooping in small containers. She would defecate in waste paper baskets, Marriott coffee cups, and bowls were a favorite—even in the bathroom sink; anywhere, but the toilet.

Her family had been notified that she was being asked to leave, but somehow she never was evicted from Room 606. The maids endured the princess's poop, and I continued to listen for updates each night. (The things we do when we find ourselves without HBO...)

Then my mom was passing through town on her way to Wisconsin and stopped to visit for the night. We went out for dinner, walking the few short blocks to one of our favorite establishments. By the time we arrived back at the hotel, we had imbibed a little wine and were feeling no pain. My mom had to get her suitcase out of the car so we headed downstairs to the underground garage, giggling all the way.

To this day I cannot remember for the life of me what we were laughing about, but it didn't stop, only growing more contagious and uncontrollable. Then it happened; my mom peed. Now I'm not talking a dainty drop here and there; no, I'm talking about a flood! It was endless, like the *Energizer Bunny*, it kept going, and going...

How I was going to get her upstairs, without my nightshift friends wanting introductions, I hadn't a clue. Thank God the hotel laundry was located on this level, and a fresh load was pressed and folded; stacks of towels were all ready for the maids come morning. Genteelly, my mother wiped and courteously recycled her used towel in the *Dirty* laundry bin, but there was no cleaning up her puddle...*Hell, it was more like a lake!*

The following evening, as I greeted the night crew, I settled in to hear all the "news."

"The maids are pissed!" someone said. "Room 606 has gone too far this time..." another rumbled.

Apparently, *Doo Doo Deb* went downstairs last night and urinated all over the garage. She even peed inside the *dirty* laundry bin (they exaggerated).

"Ew," I replied, trying not to burst out laughing.

"So what did you do last night, Lee?"

Shit!

Oh Brother, It's Aunt Boobie

At twenty-six, I played golf regularly, had a Pro named Bernie, and enjoyed opportunities to attend PGA events. A popular sport amongst my family, I was a regular at the driving range, but my understanding of the game was just beginning.

Attending one of my very first tournaments would prove to be an experience that unfortunately left an impact, and remains not only with me, but also with my brother to this day.

My instructor, Bernie, was a retired professional caddy for the LPGA and had toured in the seventies with a family friend and *Hall of Famer*. In his sixties now, he sported an extra forty or more pounds and a moderate case of *Rosacea*. There were several family members concerned about his intentions toward me, but Bernie was just about as dangerous as he looked; it wasn't Bernie who I needed to be leery of.

Golf is a predominately male-dominated pastime, so most females will garner a good amount of unsolicited attention. Being young, blonde, and in the company of an older man will get you oodles of ogling; this was something I wasn't prepared for.

Walking with Bernie into the Clubhouse, I expressed my annoyance. As we proceeded to the pool deck for refreshments, I complained about all the "dirty old men" gawking at my chest.

"Do they not realize I can see them staring?" I stated irritably.

Developing overnight at age twelve from a training bra to a 34-E left me with a very mature figure for my age. I learned early on about men's tendencies to stare, drool, and stumble over themselves because they see BOOBS!

Just then, a group of three approached Bernie and me. It just so happened to be my older half-brother, my brother's step-dad, and my nephew.

"I told you it was Aunt Lee-Lee," my nephew smugly announced.

Not even saying *hello,* and rudely ignoring Bernie as if he didn't exist, my brother's first words to me were, "What are you doing here?!"

Was he really upset because I was with Bernie? No, it wasn't that, though he made it abundantly clear how he felt about the poor guy.

Apparently, this threesome had been standing poolside, observing the "scenery," when my brother spotted something...

"Check out the *rack* on that one!"

"It's Aunt Lee-Lee," my nephew laughingly informed the group.

Yep, my brother was checking out his own sister's bosoms—and he's worried about my elderly golf pro with a skin condition!

This story is often recycled at family functions from time to time, but I don't play golf anymore...and my brother always looks me in the eyes.

Mom and the Fishermen

My mom was out of town photographing birds, when two fishermen approached.

"Will you give us a jump?" one asked.

(Their battery had died and they were hoping she could help.)

Her response: "Sorry, I'm a married woman."

Ninny

It was 1965, the Vietnam War was escalating, women's skirts were getting shorter, while men's hair length was getting longer. Martin Luther King, Jr. marched for civil rights in Selma, Alabama, and the Voting Rights Act became law.

Ninny as a blonde...because "Blondes have more fun!"

Geneva was a nineteen-year-old mother of two from Palatka, Florida. Living on the West side, in the neighborhood known as *Newtown*, Geneva married an older man and took the last name *Jones*. That wasn't to be the only big change for the young ebony-skinned bride and her children.

Tyrone Jones was a thirty-one-year-old handyman with general mechanical experience. Geneva was his second bride, and obeyed him better than the first, which pleased him. Mr. Jones excitedly informed his new wife and family to pack their belongings; he had been offered a position working for the prominent Vineyard family a few hours south and they had only two days to relocate.

"We start first thing Monday morning," he told his wife.

"We?" Geneva questioned.

"Oh, didn't I tell you?" her husband innocently began. "You will be the Vineyard's housemaid, and I will be Mr. Vineyard's chauffeur and personal valet."

Growing up in a small town in the South, Geneva was only the second-generation of *free blacks* in her family, and lived in a time with *serious* racial prejudices. If you were dark-skinnned in Palatka, you didn't cross the train tracks into the white neighborhood, or you may find yourself hung from an oak tree. Really.

The last thing this young woman wanted to do was leave her home to go clean up after some rich white family, but her husband told her she would, and so she did.

The first year working for the Vineyards was not how she had imagined it would be. Mr. and Mrs. Vineyard were kind-hearted, and fair employers. Geneva had never worked as a housemaid before and was so horrible at ironing that after burning a fourth shirt of Mr. Vineyard's, Mrs. Vineyard had her send all future items out for dry cleaning, instead of replacing her with someone more capable.

Not only were they patient with Geneva's lack of ability, but they treated her as part of the family, inviting her to share meals with them at their table. This made Geneva very uncomfortable; she didn't know what to make of these unexpectedly decent white folks, so she continued to take her meals alone, in the back of the kitchen.

One day, the Vineyard's sixteen-year-old daughter came home from school with a new vinyl record. Upon hearing the music blaring from upstairs, Geneva wandered toward the familiar sound of *Soul*. It was Aretha Franklin, and that white girl was dancing and singing her heart out. Just then, the teenager paused, spying Geneva in the hall outside her bedroom, and asked her to come in.

Geneva obeyed, but kept both eyes focused on the floor, not once looking up at the white family child, fearful of disrespecting her in any way.

"Geneva," the teen said firmly, "look at me."

Geneva timidly glanced up, but not directly at her.

"Look me in the eyes," she clarified.

The round coffee-brown oculi of the servant regarded the soft green gaze of the fair-skinned girl. She found a kind face, not a hint of anger.

"Always look people in the eyes when speaking, Geneva. You are just important as anyone else— never forget that! Hold your head high. I never want to see you looking down again." After the Vineyard's daughter finished her lecture, something changed in Geneva that would never be as before.

From then on, Geneva ate all meals with the family, sharing in their day, and familiarizing them with her own.

Tyrone Jones was a very controlling man, so when Geneva wanted to learn how to drive a car he said, "Absolutely not!" Now, Mrs. Vineyard was not your meek, abiding, fifties housewife, so when she heard of Geneva's desire to learn, she bought a car registered in her name, and paid for private driving lessons.

Geneva would tend to the house while the family was away during the summer months. Wanting to be sure not to kill Mrs. Vineyard's plants, which was something else unfamiliar to her, she began enquiring about basic plant care. Anxious that her nonexistent green thumb would disappoint her employers, Geneva thought to herself, *What would Jesus do?*

Concluding that Jesus would pray, Geneva knelt over Mrs. Vineyard's greenery and began.

"Dear Lord, don't you die!"

Geneva's daily devotional with the Vineyard's house plants included the repetitive mantra, "Dear Lord, don't you die!"

When the family returned home from vacation two-and-a-half months later, the plants were thriving.

"My plants look beautiful, Geneva!" Mrs. Vineyard was genuinely impressed.

"I heard they like it when you talk to them, and *butter my buns,* I believe they enjoyed our conversations," Geneva proudly volunteered.

When the Vineyard's daughter got married and had children, Geneva was there, however she was now called "Ninny," named by the Vineyard's first-born grandchild. And when the second baby arrived, Ninny became an honorary surrogate mother to the little girl.

Ninny and me (1976)

When the child was in third grade, her parents went on vacation, leaving her and her sister with a family member from their father's side. Mr. and Mrs. Vineyard were on a trip of their own, and therefore unavailable to chaperon their granddaughters.

The rotten relative babysitting the girls never had children of her own, and never wanted any; she despised the lesser, more inferior traits of a naturally developing juvenile. She was set in her ways about blacks, too. Ninny worried helplessly and felt bad for her babies. She called and offered her assistance to the spiteful sitter, but all she got was a hang-up and dial tone as an answer.

The youngest became very ill, but was sent off to school anyhow. Here was a middle-aged woman who allowed small children to stay up late during the school week to watch the mini-series, *Hollywood Wives*, just so she had someone to discuss it with.

Then she sent a minor in her care to classes with a 104-degree fever. Ninny was confident the girl's parents would be horrified if they knew what was happening, so when she received a phone call from the middle school's nurse's office, she immediately took action.

The littlest one, Miss Lee, was burning up and needed to be home in bed. The school nurse had called the sitter to come pick her up as there was still over four hours left in the school day, but she refused.

"Call Ninny," the child weakly told the nurse.

As Ninny pulled in, putting the car in *PARK,* Miss Lee thanked her profusely and begged her not to go. At that point, the front door opened and a masculine Italian woman came marching out.

"I told the school she was to stay there until the bus picks her up at the end of the day. How dare you go against my authority! Her parents left *me* in charge, not some *nigger* maid!" she boomed at Ninny, who was sitting in her car with no visible reaction or clear expression distorting her lovely features. I, however, was terrified, not to mention extremely ill.

"No, I called Ninny," I confessed. "It's my fault," I finished weakly.

"You better hope to God you really have a 104-degree fever, or I'm taking your butt right back to school," the *dragon-sitter* hissed behind her razor-sharp fangs.

To Ninny she said, "You, get out of here before I call the cops."

"Don't be mean to Ninny...No, please Ninny, don't go!" I remember crying as she backed the car my grandparents bought her out the driveway.

Rounding my street corner, windows rolled down, and the voice of Aretha Franklin blaring, demanding *Respect*, Ninny called out...

"Negroes — Sweet and docile,

Meek, humble and kind.

Beware the day

They change their mind...!"

I didn't fully understand it at the time, but what I had witnessed that day in my front yard was racism at its ugliest. Geneva Jones quoted Langston Hughes in retaliation to such heinous bigotry; for me, hers had been the greater lesson that day. The entire experience impacted and inspired my budding consciousness; determining the direction of my developing moral compass.

As my mother had taught her, she showed me:
always keep your head high, respect and know your
self worth, and never allow anyone to force your
eyes to the floor.

*Ninny attending my high school graduation was not only a
complete surprise, but meant the world to me.
(Graduating Class of 1994)*

He Died?!

*Mommy photographing wildlife while Rudder
(Portuguese Water Dog), her dedicated and constant companion,
oversees her every move*

My mom is a wildlife photographer and has traveled all over the world. She has photographed grizzly bears in Alaska during the salmon run, blue-footed boobies in the Galapagos, and the *Big Five* in Africa (African lion, African elephant, cape buffalo, African leopard, and rhinoceros), just to name a few.

One trip to Montana proved to be especially precarious while she was photographing mountain lions. One male aggressively came barreling through the river to where my mom was on the other side. The cat pounced, landed on her foot (breaking it), then playfully attacked her backpack. Just as quickly as the animal had arrived, he was gone.

My mom was fine, except for the shredded side of her bag, and a broken foot for a "war wound." Unfortunately, the entire family was going to Las Vegas for my stepdad's birthday in a week, and my mother couldn't walk. She had just returned from safari, and her doctor restricted her from any weight-bearing on her right leg.

Ever the positive problem solver, she purchased a new device on the market called a "knee scooter." My mom ordered the upgraded, more expensive *off-road* version, thinking of the various types of terrain and its overall stability. What she ended up with was a clunky, heavy, contraption that was impossible to maneuver.

Our trip to Las Vegas went something like this:

Walking the strip, *Where's mom?*

Huffing and puffing, trying to keep up half a block behind.

In line at the buffet, *Where's mom?*

Excusing herself as she repeatedly bumped into the backs of occupied chairs, treading on countless diner's feet, and still not even remotely buffet bound!

My poor mother was struggling. While she was paying for this entire birthday celebration, she was literally being left in the desert dust. Still, she remained remarkably determined to keep up.

We were staying at the Mirage Resort and Casino, where Siegfried and Roy had their show and White Tiger Habitat on display. Less than a year prior, Roy Horn had been attacked and left partially paralyzed. As our family was walking through the exhibit, my mom was twenty feet behind us, scooting along as fast as she could.

I was talking to my sister and made some joke pertaining to Sigmund Freud's *Oedipus Complex*, and the discussion went deeper, concluding with the founder of psychoanalysis's death. My mom came rolling up, hearing only the last parts of our conversation.

"He died?" she exclaimed.

"Yes, he's been dead like, forever," I said, trying to figure out with whom she was confusing Freud.

"Oh, no!" she finished miserably.

That's when I realized...

"Sigmund Freud, NOT Siegfried and Roy!"

Sigmund Freud (1856-1939)

Awaiting our return flight home, the family dilly-dallied, eager for our mom and her ATV to get through the security checkpoint. My stepbrother had lent me the classic novel, *On The Road*, to read. As I was returning it to him, my mom came wheeling up.

"Did you know he died in St. Petersburg, Florida?" I said to my brother.

"Who?" Mom asked.

"Jack Kerouac," I said.

"He died? Oh, no!"

Dear Lord, who was she thinking of now?

"Mom, he's been dead since before I was born," I slowly replied.

"Oh" was all she said, but her expression could not hide her confusion.

"Who are you thinking of?" I challenged.

"The chef that travels all over the world—the unappealing one with tattoos," she offered.

Anthony Bourdain

"Anthony Bourdain!" we all hooted with laughter.

"He's still alive," I reassured her in between giggles.

My mother, fed up with being laughed at and left behind (on the trip she funded!), turned to her family and broadcasted, "Well, did you know *Barbaro* died?"

*Barbaro Memorial Statue
(Churchill Downs—Louisville, KY)*

Most of us knew of the American thoroughbred racehorse who won the Kentucky Derby, but shattered his leg two weeks later in the Preakness Stakes. We were all pulling for the horse since his injury the prior year. The news was heartbreaking and I couldn't help myself.

"He died?" I questioned my mother; all eyes were on her.

"Yes," she said smugly, satisfied that she knew something we didn't.

"Oh, no!" I responded automatically without thought.

Turning her scooter toward our departure gate and pushing off with her left foot, she looked over her shoulder at her family and declared, "Let's go, slow pokes!" And with that my mom took off, downhill, through *Gates A-C*. For the first time since landing in the Mojave Desert, we were the ones unable to keep up; left behind in the dust of my mother's all-terrain scooter.

The Golden Years

Introducing Mr. and Mrs. Vern and Janet Vineyard!
(Wedding date—June 23, 1945)

Amah and Ampa were my maternal grandparents. I witnessed their evolution as they aged. I had heard stories from my mother about how they were as folks, which was quite different from my experience as their granddaughter. However, as an adult, watching my grandparents navigate the "golden years" impacted and left me with the foresight of my own future geriatrics.

Amah did not age like Ampa; Amah was always graceful and fun; the life of any party, she never turned into a typical "old lady." Nevertheless, she often had difficulty with the latest technology and terminology, which was not her forte, but didn't stop her from trying.

My grandmother, Amah

For example, I met a boyfriend on eHarmony and introduced him after several months of dating. My grandmother liked him immediately and remarked with astonishment: "It is just amazing what you can find on eBay!"

I had to explain the difference between eHarmony and eBay, but she continued to confuse them anyway.

Amah's biggest grievance with aging was the passing of all her dear friends, but Ampa's "maturing process" was more conventional.

Ampa had been a powerful businessman, nationally respected, as well as an expert and professional influence to those in his field. After he retired, he was still a formidable man, with the wits of a twenty-year old.

Unfortunately, he was diagnosed with oral

Ampa (Bayfield, WI—1984)

cancer at sixty-eight years old and part of his tongue had to be removed. Even after years of dedicated speech therapy, my grandfather never fully recovered.

I watched him struggle. I watched as peers no longer asked for his advice or opinion, ignored him, assuming he was incompetent. I watched my strong, powerful grandpa disappear, become a shell of his former self. Over the next twenty-two years, I continued to observe Ampa's metamorphosis.

Ampa (1986)

Most elderly are likened to babies; they are bald, wrinkly, and need a diaper most of the time. Watching loved ones age is not exactly enjoyable, but it can definitely be entertaining (if your funny bone is bent like mine is, anyway).

As Ampa got older and started to shrink, his clothes stopped fitting correctly. He had no intention of investing in any new outfits, nor of looking ridiculous in his extra-baggy ones. At his second home, in Northern Wisconsin, he discovered a preferable way of shopping. Ampa would go downstairs to the guest room closet, a.k.a. Uncle Flip's room, where his options for garments were endless.

My uncle would come to town and look for apparel he had left in his room for when he returned. My grandfather fibbed to his son when asked about his missing items.

"Huh? No idea where your slacks went...I haven't seen that shirt you're speaking of—ask your mother."

Sure enough, my uncle would ask my grandmother, who went to look for the missing garb, which were discovered hanging in Ampa's closet. Amah would give Uncle Flip back his threads; however, the same day he'd leave town, Ampa would be back downstairs shopping through his son's wardrobe.

"I love that shirt, Ampa. It looks great on you." I'd compliment him on a piece of clothing and the reaction was always the same from then until the day he passed away.

"Thank you," he would say, his eyes twinkling with laughter.

My grandmother would interject annoyingly, "It's your uncle's shirt! Your grandfather keeps stealing his things." I would catch Ampa's eye and return the twinkle of amusement.

Ampa had scoliosis and doctors believed acupuncture could help. My mother found a wellness clinic for him to go to while up north for the summer. The practitioner was a Doctor of Osteopathic Medicine, specializing in TCM (Traditional Chinese Medicine). The physician also had a pet she brought with her everywhere—including work.

As Ampa and my mother entered the small cabin converted into a doctor's office, they were greeted by the practitioner's four-legged companion, Maicoh.

Standing in the hallway, head low, and eyes glowing, was Maicoh in her inhospitable "welcome" stance. Immediately, Ampa shoved my mother in front of him, and steadily forced her forward with his walker.

"That is NOT a dog," Ampa nervously announced. "You go first," he urged my mom.

The doctor came out and introduced herself as Dr. Yepa (Native American for *snow woman*), and then officially introduced her pet, Maicoh (*wolf* in Navajo).

Ampa was correct, this was not a dog, but a full-grown, pureblooded female wolf that he had tried to feed his daughter to!

Eventually, like most older seniors, Ampa had to cease operating a motor vehicle—thank God! Yet he continued to fight for his independence, so when the DMV (Department of Motor Vehicles) license renewal notification arrived in the mail, Ampa was determined.

"Your reaction time isn't what it used to be, daddy," my mother gently tried to explain the logical reasoning for why he shouldn't be behind a wheel.

"It's not like your reflexes are that much better than mine. You're old too, ya know," my grandfather retaliated.

"The DMV wouldn't have sent me a notice if they didn't think I could drive. Dottie will take me down there tomorrow," he finished.

Dottie had been my grandparent's housemaid and nursemaid for the last six years of their life. Dottie was wonderful with them, especially my grandfather who was more stubborn than most. Gathering Ampa's walker and wheelchair, Dottie loaded him along with his lumbar support pillow and a can of *Ensure* into the car, and off to the local DMV they went.

"Vineyard," the clerk called his name, and five minutes later, with the help of his walker and dear Dottie, my grandfather eventually made it to the window.

"Sir, how can I assist you today?" the clerk offered. Pulling out his crinkled letter, he handed it to the girl behind the counter and confidently confessed that he was there to renew his driver's license.

The attendant tried to explain that whether you are currently driving or not, the state mandates you have a license for identification purposes; the renewal notice was not necessarily for driving privileges. Not giving up, Ampa continued, and kindly, she humored him.

After passing his eye exam, Ampa was halfway to freedom, until the "motor skills" part.

"Do you always require a device for assistance walking—such as a wheelchair, walker, or cane?" the clerk inquired.

"Yes, all of the above,...but only for long-distances," Ampa fudged the last part. Who he thought he was fooling I'll never know, especially since the attendant had just witnessed his lack of mobility.

"As long as Dottie helps me get behind the wheel, I'm sure I could drive," Ampa said hopefully.

Leaving the DMV, Dottie helped Ampa into the passenger seat, and then safely drove him home. Voluntarily surrendering his driver's license and replacing it with a state identification card was to be their little secret. As far as the family was ever to know, Ampa aced his Supplemental Driving

Performance Evaluation test, and was just pacifying everyone—including all permitted motorists, by allowing Dottie to chauffeur him about town.

Suffering frequent mini strokes, confusion became an acute issue for Ampa during the end of this life.

One day while Dottie was cleaning the kitchen and Ampa was watching The Weather Channel (his favorite), she heard him yell out for her.

"Dottie...Dottie!" Ampa hollered from his leather reclining chair in front of the television.

As Dottie rushed into the living room to find out what was wrong, Ampa continued, all flustered.

"Dottie, I'm burning up!"

Clearly concerned, Dottie hurried to Ampa's side. "Your head is as cool as a cucumber," she related.

"Dottie, I tell you I am on fire! Look, I'll show you." Pointing to the top left corner of the television screen he said, "There, do you see?"

"It is 152 degrees in here!" he continued in a panicked tone.

"That is not the temperature, that is the station channel number," she reassured him.

Poor Ampa. Facing those last seasons of life isn't for sissies. You say goodbye to friends and family, along with your control of bodily functions. You no longer recognize the person in the mirror, but that's okay because you can't see anyway. However, your *golden years* can still be one of joy and fulfillment.

As I wander the autumn of my life, I hope I become even more crazy and care-free. I intend to wear bunny slippers and push my pet pig around Walmart in a baby stroller.

I want to use the excuse that I have been here longer, therefore I am entitled to move slow, ask a lot of questions, bitch about the "kids" these days, complain about the weather, and reminisce about how things once were.

I welcome senility; I welcome it all. And when I take my last breath, I pray it will be peacefully in my sleep; but if not, I hope I die laughing.

Amah and Ampa (1985)

You know you are well on your way

to Grey Gardens

when the only one finishing your

sentences is your mother!

Mommy Dearest

Mommy (9 months old)   *Mommy (1950)*

My mother has always been the one I love most, the one I am closest to. I write a lot about her because she is a big part of my life, and constantly makes me laugh. She insists I get my sense of humor from my father and her mom, but the truth is that I am more my mother's daughter than anyone else's.

I am the woman I am today because she led by example, showing me the way. When I was in first grade, I was given my earliest writing assignment. The topic: *Who is your hero?* That was easy—I wrote about my mommy, while the other children chose fictional characters like Superman or Barbie.

Mommy—always a lover and protector of 'beasties' big and small
(1950)

I was an intuitive and sensitive kid, what my mother called "an old soul." Since birth, I worried about other people's happiness—my mom's most of all.

So one day when my dad was out of town on business, my mother, sister, and I went to the beach to play in the sand and surf. I think I was only three at the time, but I recall that I didn't want my mommy to be lonely. As my older sister quietly sang songs to herself, building her own sandcastle with an extremely large, impenetrable mote, and my mom sunbathed in her itsy-bitsy bikini, I headed down the beach on a mission.

Mommy (Mexico 1983)

Bad taste in men even back then, I discovered a man forty years my mother's senior that struck me as a good companion for her. He wore leopard bikini bottoms and a medallion on a gold chain around his neck. (Looking back, it was probably the necklace that attracted me; I love sparkly things.)

123

"My Daddy's away on business and my mommy's lonely; will you come keep her company?" Never giving him a chance to respond, I grabbed his leathery hand and led him over to my oblivious mom.

Understandably, she was horrified, just as he was understandably flustered. I stood as my mother firmly gripped my hand to keep me next to her, but my eyes followed the leopard spots as they hurried away.

My mom always said she had to dress me in the brightest colors so she wouldn't lose me. After that day, she threatened to get a leash for me, too.

As a hormonal, clueless, insecure little darling (a.k.a. a teenager), I came across an old fabric

Me—unleashed!
(Wisconsin 1979)

notebook full of poetry; it was my mother's from college. Not only did it inspire me to write, but it taught me as well.

Mommy's authentic college notebook

When I was older and she was miles away on an overseas trip, we communicated our daily highlights through emails. She would have me laughing my ass off, and in return, I found my *authentic* writing voice through correspondences back to her.

She has heard every story I have ever written, continuing to remain my biggest fan and best critic. She has been a confidant and a source of wisdom. A selfless goddess of care and giving, a brave warrior of strength—my mother encompasses these traits, and showed me her greatest example of grace early one morn.

My father passed away when I was fourteen, so my fifteenth birthday was the first without him. My mother gave me my presents before school that day. It was the beginning of many times to come that I opened a card and all it said was, *Love, Mommy.* The silence of the blank space next to hers was deafening.

Daddy (Summer 1986)

I don't recall every gift I received, but I remember looking at my mom and watching her struggle; she tried so hard to make that day as wonderful as the last fourteen.

Even though I could sense the cement block in her stomach, and see the loneliness in the lines around her eyes that spoke of another sleepless night, I watched her hand gently rest on her thin, but perfect lips, and saw my mommy smiling.

I often wonder if she realizes that on that early morning, she gave me the greatest gift of all that I still carry with me. That woman, who was my first hero, my best friend, and inspiration, taught me what it was to have strength and courage.

I read a research paper proving that if you reach out and call people they will live longer; so I make sure to talk to my mom every day—or more. Because life without her would be like a broken pencil—pointless.

Postscript: As you now know, I share everything with my mom, including this, _her_ story. After reading it, this was mother's response:

> _That's it; you don't have any_
> _more wonderful things to say about me?_
>
> _I like it when people see the nice things you write_
> _about me;_
> _it's a real 'feel good.'_
>
> ~ Mommy

Mommy and Rudder—
her badass
Portuguese Water Dog
_(2015)_

When life throws a curve ball...duck!

Curveball Confessions

Confession session

The Science of the Shopper's Cart

Do you ever eavesdrop on other shopping carts while waiting in the check-out line? I do. I also *try* not to judge or make assumptions when I see certain products being purchased. Yet I can't help but see a story everywhere I look. (That's just what I do.)

Like the overweight gentleman buying the *family size* macaroni and cheese, a 24-pack of *Charmin Sensitive Mega Rolls with Aloe*, and maximum strength laxatives. Then there is the young hormonal female in the Express Lane with nothing but a box of tampons and a dozen chocolate cupcakes with sprinkles. It doesn't take much imagination to figure out what the college student has planned for his evening's entertainment with his purchase of *Boone's Farm Strawberry Hill* wine, a pack of decent sized *ribbed for her pleasure* condoms, and a single wilted red rose suffocating in cellophane.

Yes, you can definitely surmise a lot about a person from what they buy. Knowing this, you would think I would be more conscious and aware of the story my shopping basket may be telling. Sadly, this was not the case, as I found out one rainy, Saturday night.

I went to Walgreens to pick up a prescription that had been ready since Thursday. I needed to grab a few other supplies, so I threw on a low profile ball cap, opened my umbrella, and headed out into the mugginess of the unrelenting evening showers.

I had been coming to this location since I moved to the area a year earlier. Most of the employees knew me on a first name basis by now; however, the weekend nightshift workers were unfamiliar to me.

Parking my cart alongside the pharmacy register, I spelled my last name and confirmed my date of birth for the handsome technician.

"Would you like to pay for your stuff here?" The baritone of his voice made me pause before answering.

"Yes, please," I smiled coyly at him.

As he rang up the few items I was buying, he repeatedly looked at me, flashing a brilliant smile, and then continued scanning. I couldn't tell if he was flirting or *high*; he seemed more amused than anything, which I found unusual.

Placing my prescription on top of my purchases, he handed me the bag saying, "Now you have a good night," ...and winked.

It was bizarre: I couldn't explain it. The way or tone in which he said, "...have a good night," was odd, like I was missing the punchline of a joke—and the joke was on me.

The five minutes it took me to get back home were absorbed in deep thought and self-examination. As I unlocked my front door and stepped inside, I put my Walgreens bag down on the dining room table, and began to unpack my purchases when... *OMG, OMG,...OMG!*

Mystery solved.

When item number three was revealed, after item number two, well, let's just say there was a pattern.

Item #1: Prescription refill—for birth control pills

Item #2: Batteries—for one of those electric ab toning belts

Item #3: Lube—for the worthless electric ab toning belt I bought off an infomercial at three in the morning!

Item #4: Blank VCR tape—for a movie I was tapping off HBO (back when we still used videocassettes)

And finally...

Item #5: One can of Red Bull Sugar-free—for the energy I'll require in getting across town to a different drug store for all future prescription needs.

What doesn't kill you,

makes you wish it did!

My Adventurous Stay
On Amity Island

*JAWS Attraction
(Universal Studios)*

My sophomore year of college, I worked as an actress at Universal Studios (Orlando), killing the shark at *JAWS*, forty-eight hours a week.

JAWS is located in the section of the park called *Amity*, after the fictional town from the film. When you arrived on *Amity Island*, it is as if you walked into the movie, as with most of Universal Studios. However, at certain times of the year, the

Amity Island (Universal Studios)

entire illusion of the park is altered to fit whatever after-hour festivities are planned.

During the month of October, Universal has their annual Halloween event called *Halloween Horror Night,* when the streets come alive with roaming creatures, terrifying haunted houses, "Scare Zones," live music, and all the rides remain open and operating.

On duty at one of these after-hour parties was in completely contrast from your typical shift, and it did not take long to figure out the distortion was due to the amount of alcohol consumed by guests.

Working one of the very first *Halloween Horror Nights,* Shaquille O'Neal, an up-and-coming basketball player making a name for himself with the local NBA team (Orlando Magic), showed up with some friends and family to ride *JAWS.*

Stationed in *VIP* that evening meant I was to escort "backdoor" pass holders to the front of the line and onto the next available boat. As Shaq and his entourage entered the attraction, inebriated fans started pushing their way toward him—and it was also in my job description to protect him.

Standing in front of Mr. O'Neal, guarding him from any unruly guests, I looked over my shoulder and assured him by declaring, "You'll be fine; I got your back." To which he responded with booming, baritone laughter.

I am five-foot, three inches, and as I looked into his kneecaps, and then continued to raise my eyes up, up, all the way up to his face, his expression clearly reflected his amusement with the situation.

Just then, a Shaq supporter stumbled forward and through the closed gate. My beloved basketballer physically picked me up and placed me safely aside, simply saying, "No, Lil Mama, I got this."

I suppose, as I sized up all seven feet, one inch of him, he was probably right; he was capable of taking care of himself, and didn't require my *muscle* that evening after all.

Shaquille O'Neal

While *Halloween Horror Nights* are the highlight of the fall season, *Mardi Gras at Universal* is the party of the year. It is the younger, hotter sister to New Orleans festivities, with a dazzling parade, Cajun cuisine, live concerts, and 32 oz. classic *Hurricane* cocktails. It is one huge, ongoing celebration kicking off in February and lasting until the end of March.

One night, while the festival was in full-swing, I habitually navigating the dark waters of *Amity,* with a boat full of wildly intoxicated passengers. After completing the third scene, *JAWS* made his first visual debut. That's when a woman, located in the second to last row, decided to take off her top and jumped from the vessel to swim with the shark (a.k.a. *JAWS).* On nights like these, I needed to add to my welcome spiel: "Keep your arms, legs, as well as your entire body—including both breasts---inside the boat at all times..."

The attraction immediately shuts down as a safety precaution anytime anything (or anyone), enters the water due to the hydraulic sharks, mechanical tracks, and other dangerous features beneath the murky surface.

Waiting for the technicians to reset the ride so I'd once more have control of the craft, I radioed for security to come fish the swimming topless tourist out of the water's of *Amity.*

While sitting in the dark, in the middle of the lake, with no power to my boat, I naturally became nervous. I was stalled only two scenes away from the end, the group was becoming agitated and uncooperative, and security was moving slower than my broken-down boat.

That is when the scrappy man seated in the first row grabbed me by the collar of my peacoat and fought for the grenade launcher I had been instinctively clinging to closely—my prop to "kill the shark." Hitting the man in the chest with the butt of the weapon, I was able to knock him backwards, but he still wasn't fazed due to his level of inebriation. Only nineteen, and I suddenly realized I was going to die at work, on a disabled watercraft, in the middle of an amusement park!

All that movement must have caused a "movement," because my assailant urgently announced he had to poop; off the boat and into the water he went, following the topless tourist.

Again, I radioed for security.

"*Mayday! Mayday!* Tower, this is vessel number two requesting immediate assistance. What is security's *20*? I now have TWO passengers in the water! *Copy. Over*," I shouted into the staticky black box.

"*Roger. Stand-by*. Did you say, *two*?" Tower immediately responded.

"*Affirmative!* And one is currently having a bowel movement on the shoreline. *Over and Out*," I winced painful, hearing my radioed reply.

After Tower heard a guest was defecating on the shores of *Amity*, security was on the scene directly thereafter.

When I first started working at *JAWS*, I was warned by the veterans to take care of my voice. At the time, more than half of my coworkers had some sort of throat malady like vocal cord nodules and polyps, vocal strains, and chronic bronchitis. It wasn't long before I faced similar ailments.

Even to this day, I will lose my voice very easily, and it is lower and raspier then before; I sound like a smoker. Let's just say, if all else fails, I could have a career in the phone sex industry.

It was Spring Break when Steven Spielberg and George Lucas came to the park with their kids. The top three actors at *JAWS* were put on constant boat rotation until the family had visited the ride.

Finally, they arrived, and the vessel ahead of me got to entertain the children of these creative geniuses. By now, I was losing my voice, and just wanted to get off the water and take a break.

Going out back to the *Cast Only* section behind the scenes, I sat down to catch my breath when a clean-shaven, good-looking gentleman approached. Sitting down next to me, I didn't know how to be confrontational and tell him only employees were allowed back there, so instead I decided to ignored him entirely.

However, he insisted on conversing and began asking me this question and that: *Do you like working here? What's your favorite part? What are you studying in college?...* He was a friendly, inquisitive, personable guy.

Asking my name, I introduced myself by simply saying, "Lee."

Reaching his hand out to mine, he said, "Nice to meet you, Lee. I'm Steve, Steven Spielberg."

That is where it should have ended, when I should have stopped talking, but *noooooooooo.*

Known for my gullibility, I wasn't about to let some total stranger fool me as well; nope, I wasn't falling for it. Everyone knew Spielberg and Lucas were in the park, but this gentleman was younger and clean-shaven; a very nice looking man, not the short, hairy filmmaker I have seen thousands of times on television.

Debating his identity back and forth, I finished with: "...You aren't Steven Spielberg, he has a bigger nose."

Steven Spielberg

At that moment, I heard a voice coming out of the trailer behind me say, "Steve."

It was George Lucas, whom I identified immediately.

Oh dear God...

Yep, I insulted the one and only Mr. Steven Spielberg!

Did I mention I was a film major in college? *WAS.*

Later that day, my world still spinning, I began loading a boat full of hot, fraternity guys. Not totally focused to begin with—all things considered, but now I had to hold in my stomach to accentuate my waistline for this

boatload of boys...and I am terrible at multi-tasking!

Slighted Mr. Spielberg, Alpha, Zeta, Omega—oh my, suck in stomach... Slighted Mr. Spielberg, Alpha, Zeta, Omega—oh my, suck in stomach...

Slighted Mr. Spielberg, Alpha, Zeta, Omega—oh my, suck in stomach...

My mind relentlessly replayed my big-mouth blunder, the beautiful boys before me, and my bulging belly, as if to remind me, until...

I closed the gate of the ride on my head, and passed out with a concussion in front the Alpha, Zeta, Omega fraternity...unable to hold in my stomach.

An hour later I was in the emergency room getting prepped for a CAT scan of my bruised brain. Adding iodine contrast for the best possible images, they took all precautionary measures with my injury, although the only thing bruised was my pride; physically, I felt fine, except for the golf-ball sized bump on my 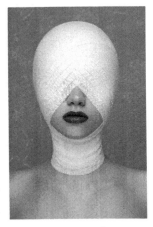 head. However, things were about to get serious.

I have very finicky veins; they are small, like to roll, and collapse when they are being poked. The nurse stuck my arms until well-perforated, trying to get the iodine dye pumping through my system. Finally giving up and listening to my incessant suggestion, she inserted a butterfly needle, and we watched as it smoothly slipped into my vein.

Irritated because the butterfly needle, normally reserved for children, is much smaller and therefore delays the dye moving throughout my system, the nurse stated she would be right back and left the room.

 She was in an awful mood due to her spring break hangover caused by too much tequila, and needed to use the Ladies Room.

Good riddance, Nurse Ratchet, I mentally cheered.

Unfortunately, as soon as she closed the door I noticed my arm was itching where the needle had been successfully inserted. The angry red line appeared out of nowhere as I started coughing—choking, actually. My throat was closing up and I was all alone.

As I laid there, certain I was dying—again, my life didn't flash before my eyes, no angel came to greet me, and there was no bright light...probably because I wasn't dead.

Alas, it was not my time to go. The returning nurse opened the door, took one look at me, and began hitting alarms and buttons on the wall, panicking as doctors came rushing forward, administering an injection of Epinephrine, Benadryl, and then Prednisone. I was experiencing anaphylactic shock due to the iodinated contrast dye—or it could've been an allergic reaction to *Nurse Ratchet.*

I retired from *JAWS,* and all theme parks in general, soon thereafter. But my year of adventures on *Amity Island* were not meaningless, without wisdom, or personal growth.

I concluded that I may not be in the same league as Shaq, but I've got my own back—at least when it comes to protecting myself from foe who have to "go."

Amity during the fire scene
(JAWS—Universal Studios)

Also, I realized I needed to focus on school, because

Lee (Kindergarten Graduation)

I didn't want to die, or work at a theme park the rest of my life—or end up as a phone sex operator. I discovered what my parents had always preached was indeed true: *Education is your most important tool*...even if I did change my major from *film* to *journalism.*

Girl Talk—Salon Style

The Hair Salon is a sacred place for women to gather, share, and discuss *life*. Walking into this *safe* place to speak freely, the salon soon becomes a sisterhood  of psychoanalysis and group therapy for the next two hours of your life. With a room full of women, it doesn't take long to get personal.

During a recent hair appointment, my fellow salon sisters included a bridal party deliberating about their hair-dos for the special day, an overly-bronzed stripper getting her nails done, and a newly-single, middle-aged divorcee with a pained look on her face as if she was getting a Brazilian rather than just foils on her head.

My friend and stylist happened to be the parlor's proprietor, and as I took my seat in her chair, I was immediately drawn into the current topic of discussion: the *G Spot*.

"Well, has he found your G-spot?" the stripper questioned the recently befriended bride-to-be.

"Yes! Oh, yes, uh-huh—I mean, he said it was the spot." The fiancée's answer went from enthusiastic to utter confusion.

Beneath the howling laughter due to the naive bride's reply, the divorcee interjected.

"My ex always had a lousy sense of direction. The bastard was convinced the G-spot was located in the back of my throat!"

With the topic taking a thorny tone, I decided to lighten things up by announcing, "I think I have a dyslexic G-spot." Having no idea what that even meant, I at least got the conversation flowing.

The stripper getting her nails painted in her chosen color, *Botswanian Booty Call* (a bold midnight blue), proceeded to enlighten the group with her past escapades and their resulting consequences.

"Blackzilla was just a fling, a casual lover from my past, but ever since Julio found out about him, he's been acting different," she complained.

How could poor Julio get over that? I wondered. I don't know many men secure enough to come after someone named *Blackzilla* (no pun intended).

Tuning out the continuous chatter for a moment, I imagined how a boyfriend would feel if I told him my previous lover was *Episiotomy Pete?*" I had to giggle with the thought of that...and then instinctively cringe.

As I rejoined the developing dialogue, they had progressed to anal sex—and bleaching. This was not the typical discussion you find at most hair appointments, but with this ensemble of interesting, dynamic females, somehow together we were limitless.

The bitter divorcee was narrating how she had been "... sodomized by that bastard on Columbus Day, 1998" and "couldn't sit down for over a week!"

The soon-to-be *Mrs. So-and-so* and her entourage looked scared to death by the thought of someone putting it in their butts (except for second Cousin Sadie who seemed interested), while the stripper knowingly laughed, gently blowing on her wet nails.

"Anal sex really isn't all that bad, some of us rather enjoy it," she said assuredly. "I, myself, have gone so far as to bleach it," she disclosed, smiling confidently.

"What the hell did you bleach?!" the divorcee shrieked.

"I happen to be a professional entertainer and contortionist, recognized nationally, and performing all over the United States," she announced proudly.

"It's just part of the job...yah know, maintenance," she ended matter-of-factly.

"Oh, my!" the blushing bride unintentionally gasped.

"You are awfully quiet; what do you think, Lee?" my friend asked as she combed through my tangled wet locks.

Good Lord!

"Well,..." I began. "My ophthalmologist told me I have very small tear ducts, which was discovered during a recent office procedure. He attempted to insert silicone plugs into my ducts, to help maintain eye moisture, and the tiniest ones manufactured were too big for me. Also, my gynecologist said I was the 'smallest' size when measuring me for a diaphragm...And don't even get me started about that traumatic constipation ordeal I endured from the prescription of Percocet I received after breaking both ankles! So, in a nutshell, I would imagine ALL of my orifices are 'petite,' and the thought of anything going the *wrong* direction, into anywhere it shouldn't, makes me incredible anxious." I saw my stylist, in the mirror, nodding her agreement.

"As far as the anal bleaching, well,...I have always been satisfied being the *black sheep* of my family—and this black sheep doesn't bleach."

I'm In the White Car
Behind the Port-O-Potty

I know people experience *déjà vu*, wear old smelly socks to insure winning the game, or think bird poop and pennies (Lincoln up) are good luck.

We've all been told not to cross paths with a black cat; however, I am not sure what it means when you live with one.

Great, so what does this mean?!
(Suncoast Portable Sanitation)

I am not one to typically ascribe extra meaning to occurrences; I just figure life is inherently strange. However, since fall of 2014, I have become way too familiar with Suncoast Portable Sanitation, as I have accompanied them along countless roadways and highways. What is the significance of finding yourself regularly following Port-O-Pottys?

As I contemplated this further, I concluded there are a lot more people pooping outside than I had previously realized.

Sitting at the left red arrow, staring up at this chalky grey box, attached loosely by thick straps (double-looped), waiting for the light to change,

I mused: *If that thing lands on me, I don't think it'll be good luck like a bird...more like Biff's crash in the movie* Back To The Future...

When the light changed I turned, continuing on the one lane road for the next three or four miles, when suddenly I laughed...*God forbid I died from a Port-O-Potty landing on me! That would be totally appropriate—and humorous.*

It could happen, too; stranger things have. (I knew a lady who was crushed when the ceiling fell on her while she was hospitalized with a broken hip!)

Of course my last words would be, *OH, SHIT!*

...but seriously, what a crappy way to die.

A College Education

Do you remember going off to college? Were you scared? Leaving for school knowing I would return home no longer a resident, but a guest, was difficult. I was very close to my mother, especially after the loss of my father when I was just fourteen.

As she drove away from my dorm, I thought, *What now? All this freedom...*As I unpacked and began decorating my room, a naked fellow went skipping past my open door, spanning the seventh floor hallway. *Was there one of those customary college keg party's currently underway?*

Getting a better look from my doorway, I quickly realized he was not a fellow student, but a vagrant who must have lived down by the river in which the school campus surrounded.

Drunk and wild, he erratically jogged down five of the fifteen floors. The sixth level didn't know if he was real or an apparition, since their floor was reportedly haunted and known for unexplainable paranormal activities. Finally, some boys from our (co-ed) dorm fondly nicknamed, *The Outhouse*—due to the residual effects from a standard impetuous weekend, escorted the derelict off the premises.

The first week was the most difficult, but it didn't take me long to make it feel like *home*.

A group of us from the *Outhouse* headed downtown to check out the city nightlife, most of us desperately memorizing our new fake I.D.'s we had just purchased for sixty dollars a piece. Having a successful evening gaining access into the world of the *21 and up*, testing our limits and tastebuds with an assortment of silly-named shots, and after experiencing our first bar brawl, we fled into the night, but we were so hungry we stopped to get some food before reaching our dorm.

McDonald's was open 24 hours, and conveniently located on the first floor of the local hospital, minutes down the road from campus. There were approximately twelve of us that arrived in a caravan of three vehicles. After parking in the empty lot, we reconvened as we entered the restaurant at 3 a.m. looking for hot greasy food.

The girl taking our order had to weigh at least 300 pounds. Along with big black braids she continually pushed out of her eyes, she wore a name tag that said, *Tiny*.

Tiny was enjoying our group as we laughed and joked, helping her shift move faster. As she was salting the last batch of our French fries, one of her big black braids fell into the mix. Horrified, I laughed as she picked up the hair extension and stuffed it in the back pocket of her black *Dickies*.

I decided I didn't want the fries, but some of the others (perhaps a little more soused than I) dug in and enjoyed their *Super Size*.

Seated at the rear of the restaurant near the open door leading into the hospital, we heard the wheels of a gurney. Our group, silently listening, watched the doorway in order to glimpse a view for the cause of the disturbing sound. Slowly it came into view.

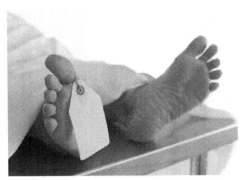 Bare feet appeared, protruding out from under a white sheet. Pushing the body was a little Latino man in his twenties, who dexterously opened the double doors and then directly disappeared.

Tiny came barreling around the corner. "Was that Jorge? He's a short, skinny Mexican?"

"I think he just went by pushing a body," someone said in shock, mirroring the emotions of the entire group.

"He works in the morgue next door," she explained.

OMG, the morgue is next door to McDonald's?

In unison, at least five of us put our sandwiches down, and then analyzed the meat.

"If you see that little *Jalapeño Popper* come back by, you tell him Tiny's lookin' for him. Can you believe he stood me up last night?" She continued her tirade all the way back to her station, behind the counter.

Most of us had lost our desire to eat; therefore, we loaded up and headed back to the *Outhouse,* deciding no one would believe this really happened come morning.

My freshman year certainly was an adventure away from home. Right before Winter Break, we had finals week. Being a private school, with an arduous academic community, anxieties ran even higher during this time. To alleviate some of the stress, Douglas McDoogle had just the plan in mind.

A medical student on a heavy dose of Adderall, Douglas broke-in and "borrowed" a cadaver from the anatomy lab. At noon the following day, above the campus quad, McDoogle climbed eight stories up the tower of the university center and announced to all gathering below: "I have had enough; I can't take the anxiety of exams anymore! Tell my parents, Dougie loves them...and that *stress is a killer!*" Then over the edge of the building went Douglas McDoogle.

Approximately one story below the top of the tower sat a small, flat cement roof, which is where he landed and had strategically arranged the cadaver the prior evening. After immediately hitting the bottom, Doug tossed the body over, so witnesses below saw it plummeting seven floors, coming to rest in the main square of campus.

To everyone's horror, they believed they had just witnessed a suicide of a fellow classmate. Even though Douglas McDoogle lived, and his plan was brilliantly executed, he was indefensibly expelled for his shameful conduct. Although no one ever saw him on campus from that day forward, he has never been forgotten by the eyewitnesses who dubbed the bizarre incident, *Distressed Dougie's Death Drop*. Remarkably, I recently happened upon Doug's *Facebook* page and guess what? Dr. D. McDoogle presently resides in Idiotville, Oregon, and is currently their Chief Medical Examiner!

College can be a tough transition, as I expected, but what I needed to learn my freshman year was not achieved in the classroom. My college education taught me that a naked man running is something you cannot ever un-see, fast food will kill you, and during times of stress, don't do a McDoogle.

Spring Break Ain't For Sissies

Spring Break has never been an enjoyable time of year for me. My first Spring Break incident happened when I was just thirteen. My sister, our friends and I went to the beach in our bikinis and newly developing girl-woman bodies. I wore a tee-shirt to cover my belly, bloated from my perfectly-timed period that arrived the first day of vacation.

As I lay there tanning, face towards the sun, knees bent, all the while holding my stomach in, my sister confronted me.

"Oh my God, Lee, close your legs!"

"Why?" I innocently answered, swiftly sitting up and immediately putting my legs together.

"You have your period," she spoke in a hushed tone.

"Yes, why?" I replied nervously.

"Your *wings* are showing, dumbass," my sister unfavorable finished.

OMG, I was laying there sunbathing with a *pad with wings* on! Worse still, my bathing suit was black and my white wings were flashing all the beachgoers. So many lessons to learn about being a woman, and so many more Spring Breaks to go.

At eighteen, I was freshly broken up with my high school sweetheart and loitering "outside the lines," when I foolishly decided to head to Daytona Beach on the back of my *new* boyfriend's *Ducati* "crotch rocket" motorcycle—unbeknownst to my mother. There was a group of us and I was enjoying my first real adventure and taste of freedom—until the ride home.

My boyfriend of two weeks told me to tap him on the shoulder should I spot a cop. Entering our county, three exits from home, I saw a State Trooper and tapped my boyfriend's shoulder. I assumed he would slow down as most normal people do, but instead he sped up.

Faster, faster, faster...the chase began and I was holding on for dear life, taking the turns and leaning in, while the aroma of asphalt and tar burnt my nostrils. The helmet was too big; I have a little head (I have been told it is comparable to an Asian's, so we know that size has nothing to do with intelligence). The strap was strangling me as we hit 175 mph, and my head was physical forced back from the wind filling my hollow helmet. *Which would snap first? My windpipe or my neck?* I wondered.

For the next eight minutes, my face forced to the sky, suffocating and struggling to breathe, I promised if I made it out of this alive, I would never jump on just anyone's *crotch rocket* again!

Twenty minutes later, I walked out of my *ex*-boyfriend's house for the last time, sporting a bruise from ear to ear. The police had finally caught up and were in the process of confronting him. I guess he had quite a reputation with local law enforcement. The last I saw of him was in my rearview mirror, the final day of Spring Break.

"S.T.O.P.

Now, some folks think when they read this on a sign that it means
- Squeal Tires On Pavement.

Other folks are mistaken to believe it means
- Stomp Toe On Pedal.

Do you know what it actually means?
- State Trooper On Patrol..."

—Officer Cerdo, Florida Highway Patrol

My last attempt to indulge in a Spring Break was nineteen years later, and guess what happened?

I was going on a cruise, stepped off an unmarked curb and fell, breaking both ankles.

No, I never cared for my Spring Break adventures, and Valentine's Day sucks too, but this *bicentennial baby* makes up for it on the Fourth of July, and at Christmas...let's just say, *this Angel already has her wings.*

Cougars, Cars, and Karma

Most of us have experienced the *walk of shame* (walking back home the day after an unplanned casual sexual encounter, dressed in the same clothes as the previous evening), but not many could relate to my version.

I was hanging out with a group of older divorcees who were wilder than this single thirty-something. Spending time with these ladies made me feel as if I needed to hurry up, get married and divorced, so that I could catch up to them.

Meeting a flock of Canadians having their annual "boys" weekend on a Saturday night at our favorite dance club, was like hitting the jackpot for these *Cougars*. Leaving my car parked in the lot behind the bar, I drove the inebriated bunch of free-spirited felines back to one of their houses, with the Canucks closely in tow.

My intention was to get a ride to my car later, but as the party pushed on, I found an empty bed in my friend's daughter's room, and passed out.

Waking bright and early Sunday morning, I left the safety of the *Princess* themed child's room to find the company dispersed, and my friend doing her usual morning *Jazzercise.* Obviously someone was feeling "refreshed."

She drove me (still in my little black dress and stiletto heels) back to my abandoned car, both of us hoping it had not been towed. As we pulled into the lot, we came to an abrupt stop, as it was blocked off.

 There was some sort of used car sale going on, and behind the crowd of potential buyers, salesmen, and inventory, was my Toyota Matrix— parked at the far back alongside a classic Volkswagen Beetle on clearance. Anxiously, I appealed to my friend.

"I can't walk through the crowd like this on Sunday morning!" I freaked.

This petite, blonde cougar courageously took control of the situation, as only a mother of four could do. Jumping out of her Suburban, she told me to get behind the wheel and drive her car, as she would be right back with mine.

Sitting in the driver seat of her vehicle was like being dwarfed in your grandfather's *La-Z-Boy*; this thing was huge. I watched in awe as my friend directed the sales people to move the barricade, explaining that her car was mistakenly parked inside.

As she approached my automobile, there was an old man guesstimating my trunk space from his view through the hatchback window. Interested  in purchasing the car, he was outraged when this young thing came out of nowhere, and was stealing it away. I watched as she nicely explained to the gentleman that the vehicle was not for sale.

Finally, she got in my Matrix and like the pro that she was, headed around the barricade and off the lot, to the old man's chagrin.

But then she saw it, or rather *him*. A sweaty twenty-something, jogging down the street. I'll admit, he was handsome and nice to look at, but he didn't distract me from driving, probably because I am not a cougar with all senses attuned for just such prey.

Overheated and currently occupied, the she-cat crashed into the back of her monster Suburban, with my tiny Toyota. Obviously, no damage was done to her vehicle, but my once immaculate Matrix was now another story.

As the crotchety old man drove off the lot in his new Chevy Malibu, he rolled down the automatic window and yelled out to my friend surveying the damage, "I love what you've done with the car!" he snickered.

Preoccupied with smugness, he drove away, almost running over the hunky jogger crossing the street. Swerving, the old man jumped the sidewalk and hit a street lamp, smashing the frontend of his new purchase.

Needless to say, with all the commotion I eventually had to show myself and get out of the rear-ended Suburban to give police reports and statements. As my friend was recapping the details to the officer, and the old man bitched about the *youth of today,* I adjusted the bodice of my little black dress and removed my other high heel.

So it wasn't your classic *walk of shame,* but standing in front of a church as the congregation is letting out, a night club at your back, and a mass of people car shopping on a Sunday morning...I decided *to hell with it,* and approached the cantankerous elder.

Walking barefoot, heels in hand, I met him at the hood of his rearranged Chevy. Looking him squarely in the eyes, I smiled and introduced myself.

"Hello, my name is *Karma*. I love what you've done with your car."

You don't have to wait for a New Year

to start a new day.

The Other Side
of the Florida Line

You know you've entered the state of Florida when you see two things while cruising the highway. For the twelve of you who have never navigated the Sunshine State, it's not palm trees and ocean views I'm speaking of.

I am referencing the famous, *We Bare All—Café Risqué*. You'll see the billboard advertisements from coast to coast endorsing, "Topless Fun," "Trucker Discounts and Showers," "Free Parking in Rear," and we can't forget their, "24 HR Breakfast, Lunch, and Dinner Buffet."

Café Risqué (Micanopy, Florida)

Yes, my foreign flock, flip-flops are all we require here in the land of sun and sand.

Another clue you've arrived in my native state are the *Silver Alerts*. No, I didn't say *Amber Alert*, I said *Silver*. If this term is unfamiliar, let me explain.

A *Silver Alert* is a public notification you'll regularly see posted on highway message signs about missing persons—usually a senior citizen with dementia.

Basically, Pops decided to say, "Screw it!," took off in the Buick, forgot who and where the hell he was, and is now cruising—Florida!

While the family is a nervous wreck and needs the public's help to locate him, Pops has found his way to *Café Risqué* and the "Early Bird Buffet." At this point, he doesn't care who he is; Pops is pretty sure he has died and gone to Heaven.

So, my fellow highway long-haulers, when you see a billboard advertising, *We Bare All*, or you are notified of a Silver Alert: *2009, white Buick, FL Tag# OUTA HRE*, don't fret. This is just our way of saying, "Welcome to Florida."

Florida Snowbirds and Lovebugs: They're Heeeere!!!

"It's fall! The leaves are changing colors....
except in Florida. In Florida, it's when the
license plates change colors."

Snowbirds are like lovebugs, and here are some reasons why:

Snowbirds are a species of human that annually migrate to warmer climates from their Midwestern tundra habitats. Heat also attracts lovebugs which arrive during the same season.

Floridian's favorite time of year is Snowbird Season— *yeah right!* Throughout the duration of this annual cycle, their

sheer numbers are so abundant in areas that it become a serious traffic hazard to anyone fool enough to take to the road; they are also an utter nuisance to Florida motorists. Congregating in unbelievable numbers along highways, they are slow-moving, especially while monopolizing the "fast lane."

Whereas lovebugs mate in flight, drunkenly wobbling around, and having no sense of direction. They can impair your vision due to their mass suicides on your windshield. Your wipers can't remove their body parts, so don't bother trying. Also, they can ruin the paint on your car, make your chrome pasty, clog your radiator, and cause overheating.

Finally—snowbirds provide a bonding banter of complaints among the locals...and so do lovebugs.

"Headline says it's snowbird season. Hey, Bubba! Does that mean we can shoot 'em?" —said resident of Polk County, Florida.

"When life hands you lemons..."

Oh, shit, I'm allergic to lemons!

Gym Etiquette: 101

If you are a friendly, smiley person like myself, then a word to the wise: *Check yourself at the door.*

As I begin my workout at the "meat market," I try not to make eye contact with the males around me. Unlike many, I am not here to meet or pick up any potential Prince Charming's.

No make-up, sweating, and contorted into some of the most unbecoming positions is not how I wish to meet the man of my dreams.

However, with females, I thought conversing would be safe. So as a perfect specimen strutted past my elliptical, with not a hair out of place and fully done up on a Saturday morning, I smiled.

"I don't swing that way, Sweetheart," was what she said!

In today's times, I worry if I say *my girlfriend* because I wonder if people think I'm talking about my lover; I have misgivings on kissing my mother in public because she may look like a *cougar*, and NOW I can't smile without some chick thinking *I want some of that!?*

While the world is "coming out," this perplexed heterosexual wants to hide in the closet. So when

I returned to the gym the following day, I naturally didn't smile at anyone.

I can just hear it now, "There's that nasty lesbian bitch."

The Kegel

Florence, my 82-year-old widowed neighbor, is in fantastic shape.

Taking her typical evening walk past my house with her two Bichons Frieses, Thelma and Louise, I commented that walking must be more beneficial than my gym membership because she looked amazing!

"No, my dear, it's not the walking. The only exercise I do is my kegels—constantly...and I have just a touch of Chardonnay now and then."

"Huh," was all I could muster.

The next morning I headed back to the gym.

The *Portofino*

I was thirty years old when I leased my first swanky, downtown condo. To go with my new pad, I decided to invest in a few brand spanking new pieces of furniture instead of keeping the mix-matched hand-me-down's from college.

Purchasing a dresser was one of the top items on my list. I went to a little furniture boutique down the road from my new home. They had a variety of options and I soon fell in love with the perfect piece.

"It's a *Stanley Portofino*," the sales gal informed me, as if I should know what that means. But I could tell by the way she said it, I should be thinking, "Wow!" And I was, but not because of dear old Stanley...I was stunned by the price for a chest of drawers, even if it was from some village on the Italian Riviera. Spending more on this one item than I had on anything in my life (other than my car), was giving me heartburn. However, when my beautiful "investment" was delivered, I could not have been happier. Fast forward three months, and

I could not have been more unhappy. My dresser began to bow in the middle. After calling the shop, explaining the situation, and emailing pictures, my dresser was decidedly "damaged" and a replacement was ordered.

Three weeks later, I received a call from the store informing me that they would be sending a truck by to do the exchange. As I cleaned out the dresser drawers, a male friend stopped over unexpectedly to visit. I couldn't very well empty my underwear drawer with him present, so I waited until he left.

My new *Stanley* was delivered and the old one taken back to the furniture warehouse. Soon thereafter, I went to shower and change clothes, and when I opened my panty drawer nothing was in there—no bras, socks, or underwear.

OMG, I left them in the other dresser!

 My distracting friend thought my situation was so amusing that he didn't want to miss one moment of it. Therefore, he willingly went to get my stuff from inside the store, as I cowered outside in the car.

Three months later, my dresser did it again. Still incredibly embarrassed, I called the boutique. "But it's a *Portofino*," the sales women on the other end exclaimed.

"What it *is*, is warped in the middle," I barked back.

Emptying the defective piece, making sure to remove all my intimate apparel this time, I found myself distracted once again. However, the delivery and exchange went smoothly, and I was soon enjoying my new *Stanley Portofino*.

Three months later, I received a voicemail from the furniture warehouse. "Ms. Volpe, you seem to have left some personal effects in the bottom drawer of your dresser we replaced a few months ago. Could you please come pick up your items?"

I didn't leave anything in there; I'm not missing anything. What is he talking about, "personal effects" in the bottom...*oh no, oh God—please!*

It could only be one thing, though my mind raced around and around like Danica Patrick, trying to find a different possible answer. Nope. My mortification set in.

Do you recall those *home parties*, like *Mary Kay* or *Tupperware*? Well, have you ever heard of *Pure Romance*? It is just like the others except instead of makeup or plastic storage containers, they display and sell *sex* products at their company home parties.

My friend hosted one once and received free supplies for being a consultant. It wasn't long before she was giving away her goodies and I was the recipient of massage oils, lube, and yes, a vibrator.

The vibrator was not inviting; enormous, veiny, and red, I imagine it must be how Spiderman's penis looks. So obvious no woman was consulted in the design phase. Well, I never used any of the items, I just kept them in a Tupperware container in the bottom dresser drawer. Believe me, if I was using all that paraphernalia, the warehouse wouldn't have had to call for me to know they were missing.

I ignored the message, blocked it from my consciousness. It was bad enough that I had done this once, but twice?

Three months later the damn dresser did it again, and you know what I did? Nothing!

How I Regained My Humor At A Funeral

As my family gathered for my step-father's memorial service, a facially-deformed gentleman approached me, introducing himself.

"Hello, my name is Jack Hoff; I was a member of your dad's poker group. Although we didn't know one another well, he was always very kind to me."

Distracted by his resemblance to Vincent Van Gogh, my mind wandered as he regaled me with stories. Before me was a man with his right ear completely removed due to cancer, along with part of his jaw. The other side of his face was severely burned and looked more like raw hamburger meat than the famous post-impressionist painter.

Still talking, Jack was getting to the part in his story which explained the cause of that particular injury.

"My wife had severe emphysema, with an acute addiction to nicotine," he recounted. "Unfortunately, the two don't mix. One evening, when I was in the garage doing some woodwork, Loretta lit up a *Virginia Slim*,  and KABOOM, just like that, she blew herself up. Now this is all I have left to remember my poor Loretta," he said while rubbing his mangled cheek.

Being overly friendly to this harmless senior only managed to get me in trouble—as it has done countless times before.

Note to the ladies: You know how men can be; you smile or happen to say *hello*, and before you know it, they believe you're flirting with them; it is so frustrating!

Note to the men: Just because a woman smiles at you, does not mean she wants to see you naked, cook you dinner, or birth your babies!

Unfortunately, this old man thought I was *interested* due to having my undivided attention. He complemented me on my "beautiful body," while salivating and managing to stare at my two breasts with his one good eye. And then he mentioned something about his "Woody Woodpecker" working like a virile sixty-year-old's

—at which point I quickly excused myself to greet other guests.

Later, as the service came to a close, my brother-in-law informed me that Jack Hoff, that notorious 85-year-old, confided in him his desire for an old, rich widow with Cerebral Palsy.

"Can you think of anything better?" Jack had said. "That way, she won't live forever, her money will support me in my final days, and when she rests her hand on my lap, it'll shake uncontrollably which will tickle my Dilly Dill pickle." Jack Hoff is a pervert—and I have it on good authority that he cheats at poker.

Postscript: A stepfather, a friend, a man of great character who completed a family that already began. I love you, Bob.

Bob and me (Christmas 2015)

There is a light at the end of the tunnel

...and it's a train!

BROKEN

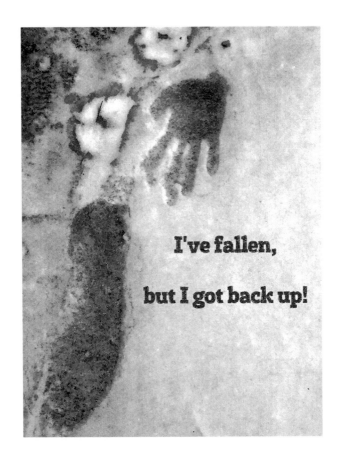

I've fallen,

but I got back up!

...3 months later, I did not!

Part One: Before the Fall

It all began in September on my 39th birthday— OMG, I discovered my first gray hair.

By evening, my day hadn't gotten any better. I told my sister I would go with her to some meeting at my niece's high school. What I didn't know, however, was we would be learning the new math curriculum they had implemented over the summer. I have a worn out *tip card* in my wallet, for Christ sakes. My dream of being the female Jacques Cousteau was shattered Freshman year of college. "Why?" you may ask. Because of MATH, that's why! So I end up spending my birthday night with my sister and an auditorium full of parents, studying a new way to learn MATH. I didn't know it at the time, but that was to be the most enjoyable part of my year...

Hello, October, and one depressed pig.

We spend our summers in northern Wisconsin, and Officer (my miniature house pig) can be as wild and free as he wants to be. Having over 80 acres to explore and an alligator-free lake to cool off in, it's no wonder he gets so down when we head home to Florida and back to life living on a golf course. This year, I had decided to do something about it.

When I returned home, after my birthday, I hired the handyman at my veterinary's office to do some minor work at my house. By October, he had brought in a general contractor to help with my "bright ideas." I had decided to extend my lanai and have pasture grass planted around the inside perimeter. I thought it would be nice for Officer; he could root and sunbathe in a more natural environment. Considering the project was estimated to take only two weeks and the price was fair, I went ahead with construction.

Bring on November, and surgery.

Diagnosed with endometriosis, I finally decided to have surgery, and was rewarded with every single complication possible. I ended up in the hospital with two blood clots and third-spacing (occurs when too much fluid moves from the blood vessels, accumulating in areas that normally have none). I did get a "lift" though; unfortunately, it was my uterus rather than my boobs or butt.

Now it's January, and the spiral continues downward.

Construction is not finished, not even close. Concrete finally gets poured and I wait, and I fight, and I wait some more. Every day is an exhausting uphill battle with one dipshit male after another. One contractor told me, "I know you want it done, but I'm pretty sure you wouldn't want a trashy job either. If I tried to explain all the inner workings and details, you'd never understand. Just sit back, look pretty, and watch me do my magic." Oh, he was *magical* all right—disappearing at 3:00 p.m., never to return.

There was always some guy "mansplaining" to me that he was giving me some great deal, or that it was supposed to look like that, and my favorite—that I would never comprehend all the reasons why they hadn't finished the job yet; these things are delicate. *Bullshit!* I call bullshit! Somehow, because I have a vagina, I can't tell that something wasn't done correctly...that this is why it doesn't look right, and that I'm being taken by a crook. As for my favorite excuse: you haven't finished the job because "my guys are fishing"!

For some reason, because I'm female, every day is like taking my car to the shop. "Is there a Mr. Volpe I could talk to?"

"Yep, you're looking at him," I said staring one shithead coolly in the eyes. The truth was, if there had been a "Mr. Volpe," I probably wouldn't be in this mess.

Now, too tired to go out with friends or be social. *What day is it?* Too exhausted to care.

February, fuck February!

The cage is still waiting to go up, and it can't. "Why can't it, Lee"? I'll tell you why, because I employed Ray Charles to pour the concrete and the pitch is off by seven inches! I also hired criminals: my recently replaced animal hospital's *jackass*-of-all-trades and his contractor/fishing buddy. Fishing: the guy is so inept he couldn't catch a shark with a severed arm for bait.

By the end of the month, I had the police, workmen's comp, and the county's code enforcement agents out at my house. The contractor was no contractor. He had provided false information, including his license number, and now the state was involved. My un-handyman got spooked and abandoned work at my property—and the state of Florida altogether. I now had to find legitimate, competent professionals to not only demolish all work that had been completed up to that point, but to begin again from scratch. I was out thousands of dollars to the *wily wankers*, and my pig had not one of the lifestyle upgrades I commissioned.

Heading into March, and Spring BREAK.

My sister, niece, and nephew were flying down to Florida, and the four of us were going on a cruise for the kids' Spring Break. I was supposed to go with them last year to New York, but six hours before I was to leave, my pig-sitter broke her ankle and I didn't have an available alternate. Last year I missed it, but this year I was determined I would not.

I employed the owner of a creditable pet-sitting company. She met with Officer several times prior to me leaving, and most assuredly supplied a substitute sitter should an emergencies arise. I was set, I was ready, I needed this: to get away from the hell I'd been in every day for the last however-many months.

In the limo, almost to the port authority, I turned to face my sister and emphasize my longing for leisure and laughter. We paid for priority boarding, so we were looking at a day on the deck, poolside, with tropical cocktails in hand. Already imagining the moments ahead, where my only dilemma was "margarita" or "mojito," I announced, "I need a break. I can't wait for this trip!"

Well, readers, be careful what you ask for. *My* God clearly has a sense of humor, although sometimes I think I've missed the joke.

Taking the last sip of water from the *Dasani* bottle, I got out of the limo and inhaled the salty air. Not wanting to leave my garbage behind, I walked across the road, stepped up on the curb where everyone was unloading, and threw my bottle away. I turned to go back, stepped down off the curb, and...there was my "trip" and my "break." *I should've fuckin' littered!*

To be continued...

BROKEN quotation #11

What comes after splat?
I'll have to let you know.

Chapter 2: After the Fall

March 28, 2016

SPLAT!

Sprawled out unceremoniously in the *unloading only* zone, I realized *I'd fallen, and I can't get up!* There had been nothing beneath my feet to support me as I descended the neglected concrete ledge. I know I saw a yellow painted railing to my left marking the cautionary curb and gutter under repairs, but I had stepped to the right of the barricade.

OMG, I'm wearing a sundress with NO bra! Horrified with the *uncensored* mental image of myself on display, in the middle of the road, exposed before God and all creation, cruise passengers, and Port Authority employees, I quickly glanced down and miraculously found I was still intact—at least there.

After barely escaping a graphic *Girl's Gone Wild* moment, I immediately directed my attention to my lower extremities—the source of intolerable, impossible-to-ignore pain. I genuinely expected my ankles to be turned around backwards, mirroring the severest of injuries endured by many professional soccer player. When I finally found the courage to peek below my knees, I was pleasantly surprised to find my anatomy appeared accurate.

Security personnel instinctively sprang into action, removing me from the path of oncoming traffic (good thinking). Suddenly, total confusion ensued while awaiting the ambulance's arrival. The *silent* alarms had been sounded, and within moments, a swarm of Port Authority *suits* came down from their upstair offices to investigate. No one wanted to talk to me; in fact, not a single soul even made eye contact. They were secretly conversing, shamelessly whispering amongst each other, all the while observing and assessing the curb in question.

Subsequently, one *suit* acknowledge me by synthetically saying, "I hear that you tripped and fell, poor thing,..." Never once coming up for air, she carelessly concluded, "...Clearly, you're a little klutzy," openly placing the blame solely at my feet. *(Yes, I know, "solely at my feet"—HA, HA, HA... Too easy; moving on.)*

"No, this was not my fault," I countered firmly. Her audacity to suggest I was somehow incompetent, thoroughly lacking the agility to even cover the span of spitting distance, infuriated me. I will have you know, I was an "early" walker. Most children start taking their first steps on their own at age twelve months, but I began at eleven. I have also been water skiing since age four, and hold the title of *Youngest Slalom Water Skier* on the lake up north, where I commonly spend my summers. Even though I refrained from enlightening the Tanya Harding of the harbor, it was for these reasons I was seething. Visibly disinterested, her silence deafening, she turned away and left the scene.

My niece proceeded to give me a pep talk. "Aunt Lee-Lee, you were so graceful when you fell—very ladylike." My nephew looked bored. My sister was on the phone with my mom catching her up on all the gory details.

Over forty minutes later, my $500 ride finally arrived. Three paramedics evaluated me, determining the urgency of transporting and admitting me to the regional emergency room. Before loading me into the back of the ambulance, I was desperate for any amount of levity, so I insisted we document my destination delay with several silly selfies. Looking back, I realize I was most likely in shock.

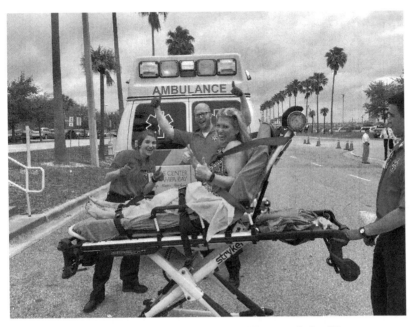

Here I am, bloodied, broken ankles...and I'm like,
"Look at me, having so much fun on my 'trip'; wish you were here!"
Seriously?! I HAVE to be in shock.

My sister was riding in the front with the driver, while my niece, nephew, two paramedics, and my broken ole self were cramped together in the back. We were having a good time, considering the situation—making jokes, sarcastically yelling at the driver for hitting every bump on the five-mile ride to the hospital—probably because we were positive I would be going on vacation.

We had paid for early boarding, so we still had several hours before we were to depart. The cruise line was aware of my situation, and they were being as helpful as possible. I looked out the back window of the ambulance and saw my ship. Quickly, I took a picture, and realized I was going in the wrong direction.

After meeting with the doctor, Radiology took me to get X-rays. Behind the imaging machine, the wall was draped with a poster of a Caribbean beach scene. After they finished taking the films, I asked if they minded taking a few more images for

...and here I am, heading AWAY from my cruise ship —and my dwindling vacation destinations.

me. Posing, as if I was laying on the beach, I had the nurses laughing while taking pictures with my camera phone. I figured with the way things were going, it was looking like this would be the closest exotic location I'd be getting to anytime soon.

"Broken. Your ankles have mirror image fractures of each tibia. We have to check and see if we need to do emergency surgery. I'm going to give you some Lidocaine in both ankles, and take you back to radiology for more images," my doctor reported. *Yep, my boat was officially docked.*

"Just so you know, Lidocaine doesn't work on me," I informed him. Evidentially not believing me, he instructed that he would still give me some. I thought the needle in both ankle joints was painful—that was until I had the scan. Lying on the X-ray machine, my doctor detailed the procedure about to take place. "Basically, we have to check ligament stability, and we do that by pulling your broken ankle as far out as possible under the imaging machine while it captures snapshots," he said. Having a high pain tolerance, I didn't think much of his words until he began. Not only was I freaking out from inhumane pain, but my doctor was disturbed and panicking as well. He'd finally realized I hadn't lied; Lidocaine really doesn't work on me.

The "radiating rays" help me to imagine I'm on a beach, sunbathing in the Caribbean.

Somehow this made me feel better, that we were both in pain, and we'd get through it together. When I arrived back in my room, my family looked shaken. They had heard me screaming from the other side of the hospital, and were freaking-out right along with me and the doctor.

We had less than an hour before the ship cast off when my doctor entered to inform us that I would not be having surgery, at this point, and I would NOT be going on a cruise either. I kissed my niece and nephew goodbye so they could hurry to catch the boat, and held on to my sister as we both cried. This was one of the worst moments of all, and the nurses felt so bad they cried right along with us.

As I watched my family disappear from sight, I lay there waiting for my legs to be cast. I don't know that I've ever felt so alone. I called my mom, who lives three hours away, to please come get me. I called the pig-sitter to let her know I wasn't going anywhere, and lastly, I called my best friend.

My best friend (BF) owned a private home health care agency. He was a highly intelligent, assertive professional, with a wealth of knowledge and connections in the medical field. After I recounted the last six hours of my life to him, he emphasized the importance of me not being discharged from the hospital. I relayed the news that they were already in the process, and my mother would be arriving very shortly.

"You can't put any weight on either foot. How are they possibly going to discharge you?" he incredulously questioned.

"A wheelchair is being delivered to the house, and I have a walker, and I have crutches too," I rallied. Honestly, I didn't know how in the world I was going to be able to pull this one off, but I preferred to be home, in my own bed, with Officer (my mini pig) and Uncle Put (my cat).

Then again, before discharge, the social worker went over all the important stuff with me, like..."So Ms. Volpe, will you have someone helping you when you return home?"

"My friend owns a home health care agency, and he is already working with my mother on setting up round-the-clock nurses," I explained.

"Until you have *home care* help, how are you going to get out of bed and transfer to your wheelchair once it arrives?" she challenged.

"I will have the chair parallel to my bed, scooch over to the side, get into a sitting position, and then transfer to the wheelchair. Done." I proudly answered.

"And what will you do if there is a fire?" she countered back.

What? WTF? "I don't know. I have a pig and a cat, and I would have to get them out, but...," I trailed off in stunned horror.

"You will crawl," she said in an apathetic tone.

Seriously? I'm not going to crawl. I have two broken ankles. I'm going to die.

(This whole "fire scenario" was to be the plot for many of my future nightmares.)

"We can't let you leave until you empty your bladder. You can either use the lavatory, or you can go in a bed pan," the nurse explained.

"Noooooo, I'll use the toilet, if it's all the same," I nearly shouted at the poor lady. Using the commode, only 6 feet away from me, was to be an incredible undertaking even I couldn't have foreseen. I have no feet, they are throbbing with pain anytime my leg/foot slightly moves, and I have the added weight of casts on top of that.

Two nurses, crutches, a walker, my mother, and the *eagle had landed*, but I couldn't pee. So I sat there, and the nurses went to go figure out how the girl with two broken ankles was going to miraculously walk. When they returned, they had news. I did too. I peed! I thought their news was less impressive. They had spoken with the doctor, who was in the process of admitting me to the hospital.

Now they want to admit me?! Not a chance. They've had all day to make that call and yet never did, but now that I've sent the pig-sitter home and mentally prepared to go, they want me to stay? "You can't even get to the toilet WITH help, what are you going to do at home alone?" the nurses drilled.

"Crawl," was my reply.

Around this time, one of the Port Authority employees delivered my suitcase to me in the hospital—with two broken wheels. Not funny!

With the help of my walker, two nurses, and my mother, they got me into the car. *See, simple.* Getting out of the car with only my mom and a walker was not so simple. As soon as I was able to reach my front door, my mother got me into a rolling chair from my patio, pushed me to my room, and deposited me in bed.

My suitcase experienced sympathy pains.

After I was able to get as relaxed and comfortable as possible, I wondered where Officer was. Uncle Put had already made himself a cozy spot next to me, and was finishing up a zealous bath. But where was Officer? It wasn't like him to not immediately greet me whenever I come home.

"Mom, can you find Officer for me?" I shouted to my mother in the other room. She found him all right, or at least the obese version of himself. She also found piles and piles of uneaten treats all over the house. Good God, that really was not like him! Pigs don't have a hypothalamus, which is the part of the brain that tells you when you are full. Therefore, he would never have left uneaten food no matter how stuffed he was; something must be very wrong.

Officer, the pig in the blanket.

With all the excitement, Officer left the den to join me in my bedroom. When I saw the size of him, my heart broke. He was in pain. The wonderful pet-sitter I hired, who was only there for six hours, overfed Officer to a dangerous degree. And with that, Officer started vomiting ridiculous piles of treats. I was always told that it's not natural for pigs to vomit like it is for cats and dogs, and I now understood. This was serious, continuing for hours, and I couldn't do anything to help. My house suddenly began to take on the look and smell of a frat party during hazing week.

...to be continued

Chapter 3: Home Health Care

A few days after arriving home from the hospital, my first scheduled home health aide arrived, laptop in hand. My mom was still cleaning up Officer's vomit, which seemed never ending as  the discovery of new piles continued. I reclined in bed unable to move. Unfortunately, it wasn't because Officer was snuggled up alongside me, while Uncle Put sat atop my head mimicking a *Ushanka* hat. No, it was my legs; I couldn't move my lower body without feeling massive pain. I was completely helpless, and at the mercy of those around me.

Uncle Put sound asleep in his usual spot —the top of my head!

My aide was busy working hard—on her online college classes! My mother put Cinderella to shame cleaning, cooking, shopping, not to mention helping me in and out of my wheelchair, to and from the bathroom, and depositing me back in bed to the awaiting pig and cat. Meanwhile, my aide, *the Student*, was getting her degree in Health Care, and her minor in Customer Relations. To be fair, she did lift her feet occasionally so my mom could clean under them.

My best friend, the company's owner, called that evening to see how my first day using his services had gone. Unfortunately, I had to tell him that my mom threw her back out, but it was all right because *the Student* just finished a class on muscle spasms and slipped disks. Needless to say, I never saw that home aide, Health Care, Customer Relations student again.

According to the schedulers working on my case, there were two reasons why they had been unable to find me adequate personal care. One—because of Officer. Most caregivers were terrified at the thought of a pet pig, let alone one that lived indoors. The second aversion was my BF, their boss. Prospective aides had been told during scheduling that I was best friends with the boss, wherein most decided to pass. However, the bottom of the barrel could care less, and that's exactly what I got, one right after the other.

My BF, however, did find the perfect employee to send over. She was a hard worker, a grandmother, and lived out in the country with her exotic animals. She wasn't afraid of pigs, and happened to be available, so he had her scheduled to arrive first thing the following morning. I was fascinated with what I had heard about her, but that's one lesson to always remember, readers—you can't believe everything you hear.

When she arrived in the morning, the nighttime aide went over my schedule, personal needs, showed her around, and discussed my injuries. She wasn't introduced to Officer until I awoke. He was always by my side these days, protecting me. When I did finally greet her, she seemed perfect, appearing gentle and kind, like the granny I expected.

In a thick Russian accent, she told me all about herself and her son. As she got to know Officer, she explained how she used to train lions and tigers in the circus. Her boyfriend, Bear, had been the bear trainer—oh my! Currently, her son was the big cat trainer, and she wanted to take me on a field trip to her home where they keep the kitties. I was actually excited about that. Everything had been going great until she helped me to the shower.

I'm a very modest person. I get embarrassed when my friends walk around naked in front of me, or when the sales lady tries to wiggle her way into my dressing room to check the fit of my bra. So when I am at the mercy of a stranger, at life's most intimate times, I feel more uncomfortable than I would on a blind date with a blind man.

Although *Grandma Tiger Lady* did help me into the shower, I didn't remove my clothing until the door closed. Sitting on my bath chair, relaxing as the hot water massaged its way down my body, enjoying the feeling of getting clean, I savored the moment. *Grandma Tiger Lady* interrupted my tranquility by saying, "I want to introduce you to my son. He'd really like you." I had to chuckle at the thought; me, broken and wheelchair bound, and the savage, wild cat tamer.

My amusement soon turned to horror. "You have a beautiful figure," she commented. "I remember when my breasts looked like that," *Grandma Tiger Lady* said.

As I looked out my foggy, glass shower door, I saw her staring at my naked, disabled body. *Help!* As I contorted myself as best I could to block her unobstructive view, she rattled on in broken English about her life with the circus, spectacular sequined costumes, and adventures in the cage with her cats. Drifting off, her gaze once again moved over my bare frame. "Ahhh, the things you must do with that body!" she said in a nostalgic tone. *Yeah, like step off a curb and break my ankles.*

A week passed and my sister and family returned from the cruise. They came to visit me before heading back home. I don't remember much, because the pain medicine prescribed in the hospital was in the process of breaking me further. You see readers,

I was constipated. The nurse that came to check in on me every few days said if things didn't "get moving," I could lose part of my colon. So, I wasn't much for conversation. This also happened to be the first day for a new home health aide, and she was certainly getting quite the introduction.

As I screamed endlessly from my bedroom, doubled over in pain from a bowel blockage—not to mention broken bones, Officer was head butting my door, desperately trying to get to me, while my sister and family found activities (far away from me) to do before their plane flight. The *New Girl* was amazing, or at least my mother kept telling me so. Soon thereafter, my mom had to take everyone to the airport, and said she felt confident I was in good hands.

By the end of the next day, life was more tolerable, and the loss of my colon was no longer an immediate danger. New Girl and I had many adventures within those first few days of her working for me. As far as I was concerned, we made it through the battle together, to fight another day. My mom had been right, she was a keeper. Before the evening aide arrived, New Girl wondered if she could ask me a question.

"Will you adopt me?" she propositioned. *What?!* I explained that at twenty-seven, she was probably too old to be adopted. Furthermore, I'm not old enough to be her mother.

Almost forty, I contemplated her proposal. There appeared to be a lot of plusses. I could have a functioning, hardworking, adult child, who was already taking care of me. Not to mention, I could feel proud that I had successfully raised a damn good kid. That was the  moment I considered the possibility of being overmedicated.

One evening when the night shift was beginning, my regular evening aide (a chain smoker from Wisconsin) was booked elsewhere, so the agency scheduled someone new. She lasted a total of five minutes before I sent her home, and canceled all 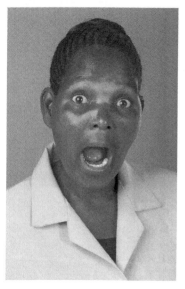 future overnight visits. *The Screamer* showed up to work expecting a guinea pig, not forty pounds of protective pork (a.k.a. Officer). She screamed, and screamed, AND screamed, and then jumped on top of me in bed, landing on both broken ankles. Naturally, I reacted by screaming myself; at which point, Officer responded by charging her like a billy goat.

I got into my wheelchair for the first time all by myself because *pork chop* had to go potty. I knew the Screamer wasn't going to be of any help, but I didn't think she would abandon her patient, either. After I let Officer outside, I looked around only to find I was all alone. My wheelchair was stuck on the track of the sliding glass doors, I couldn't move, I had to get the pig...

"Help," I yelled. Nothing. "Hello. Help!" I repeated louder and more forcefully. *Am I in some B movie horror flick?* I wondered.

Finally, the Screamer emerged from the guest bathroom, "Did you need somethin'?" *Not a thing— just wanted to say 'Hi'...*

Another memorable "worker" was sent over for the bargain-basement price of five-hundred-and-fifty dollars a day. For all intents and purposes, we will call her *Halfwit Hannity*. *Halfwit Hannity* was sweet as could be, but she never failed in messing everything up. Either she would break it, shrink it, or forget about it completely—in which case she would default to making herself something to eat instead.

Outside, on my patio was a deformed, custom gas fire pit. Thanks to the fishing buddies, it needed to be demoed and rebuilt from scratch. Containing three types of fire glass, each had to be separated and removed before construction could commence. The only thing I asked *Halfwit Hannity* to do day-in and day-out, was sort glass. Now, I did feel sorry for the poor girl...that was until I learned of her penchant for stealing silverware.

Halfwit Hannity was a pilferer. The girl was dim-witted enough to take a spoon to the Super Bowl, and I know just whose spoon it would be—mine! By the time she had finished working for me, I had one spoon, three forks, and two table knives left.

Then came *Sister*. Nearing the end of her first day at work, she wheeled me outside for some fresh air. All these gals loved to talk. I knew all about them, their mothers, daughters, husbands, lovers, lesbian partners, you name it. I welcomed the distraction. However, there were times I would have rather just focused on my all-consuming crippled ankles. While sitting outside enjoying the sunshine on my face and the breeze refreshing my hair, *Sister* started confession.

"I thought you'd be a bitch," she said, "but I'm pleasantly surprised." Surprised myself, I asked why she would think such a thing. "Because you are best friends with the boss man, and everyone hates him." Well this was getting a bit uncomfortable, but it was going to get downright alarming in five, four, three, two...

"I told the agency that you having a pig didn't bother me—if it bites me, I'll just sue you and the company.

And I don't care if you tell that good friend of yours everything I've said," she dared. "I recent got a felony assault charge on my record, and it's just a matter of time before someone finds out about it and fires me."

I just stared at her. For once in my life, words had escaped me. "You look uneasy," she observed with a sarcastic giggle. *Um, yeah...someone save me from this lunatic!*

"My sister worked for you once. She was never allowed back because of that mother of yours." *OMG, the Student; her sister was the Student!*

With the charge of "felony assault" ringing in my ears, I conceded to my present reality as a casualty of caregiver abuse and neglect. What an education I was getting; I could officially empathize with the elderly, and I wasn't even forty! Fortunately, by the end of my days with Home Health Care, I had three solid workers, two of whom I adore and I've continued to remain in close contact.

Something else that stayed with me long after my in-home care were toll tickets. I received toll violations in the mail for months afterwards. Although most aides had permission to use my car for running my errands or taking me to doctor appointments, they did not have my consent to joyride over the span of four counties and through endless toll booths. Guess who was responsible for payment? The cripple at home in bed with her pig and cat.

The Boys: Officer, the mini pig, and Uncle Put, the black cat

...to be continued

BROKEN quotation #7

One uninhibited Home Health Aide revealed her midnight musings at the start of her morning shift: "I've thought about it all night, and I just can't figure it out; how do you have sex with Officer?"

Horrified, I adamantly told her, "I do NOT have sex with my pig!"

She explained that she meant something a little different: with Officer being so protective of me, she didn't know how I could "entertain."

What a twit; I had two broken ankles and couldn't get to the bathroom by myself. The only entertainment I was interested in was *Ben and Jerry* with an anti-inflammatory on top!

Chapter 4: The Besties and the Beasties

Uncle Put and Officer hogging my king-sized bed

Now would be a good time to discuss the effects my "broken" status had on friends and loved ones. I should first explain a little about myself. I am a friendly, outgoing person, who never met a stranger. I have countless acquaintances, but allow only a few close to me. I'm stubborn, have trouble asking for help, and never want to be a bother. Being independent and living alone with a pig and a cat is all fine and well—that is, until you break both your ankles. Facing this hurdle was about to teach me not only about myself, but those I held dear.

I will begin with my four-legged children. I honestly believe Uncle Put, my black cat, thoroughly enjoyed my "handicapped" status. I was constantly in bed for him to lie on and he loved attacking and eating my physical therapy tools. But his favorite was my wheelchair; he was always curled up on

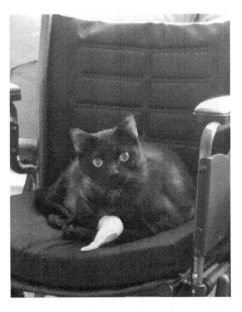

Uncle Put (and his catnip banana) atop his throne —a.k.a. my wheelchair!

top of the seat cushion as if it was his throne. I swear he went through a mourning period when the wheelchair was no longer needed and was returned. All the nurses and home aides loved Uncle Put, and Uncle Put loved all the attention. This was not the case for Officer, my mini pig.

Officer did not like the idea that Mommy was hurt and there was a revolving door of strangers coming in and out of our home. His personality changed with the snap of my ankles. He took on the role of protector—and enforcer. If my nurse or physical therapist made me cry out in pain, Officer charged. If I was sleeping and anyone got too close to me, Officer charged. He would guard my bedroom, not allowing anyone in, and if they did, he would charge. He was becoming a real pain in the *pork butt*!

I finally had to get a gate to lock him out of my room so the nurses could come in an assist me. My aides would carry a bag of treats to manipulate him with food. After he ate the treats, he would charge. Now, he never hurt anyone—that wasn't his intention; he wanted to scare the hell out of you, and that's exactly what he accomplished.

My mom had been a constant presence, comfort, and help during this time, but by the end of my second month of immobility, she had to leave town. Hers had been the only familiar face I'd seen in all that time, and I was going to miss it desperately. I had a few people reach out, which I will always appreciate, but it was my closest friends I wanted. One of those friends showed up.

Every week he (let's call him Greg) would come visit, bringing me Starbucks or some other treat, and be ready to watch another movie. Twenty-four hours a day I was at the mercy of strangers. I was so lonely; I needed the company of those who knew me best. And every time Greg showed up, I was the happiest girl in the world!

One time he came over and was wearing a back brace. He threw his back out weightlifting and could hardly walk. The two of us made quite a pair; I'm not sure which one was more disabled. I was in bed, obviously, and unbeknownst to him, Officer was sound asleep under the covers. As we chatted, he sat down, and time flew.

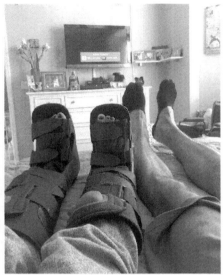

The barista's at my local Starbucks sent me a special message... and it made me happy!

My friend and movie partner

When it was time for Greg to leave, he gently got up, safeguarding his lower back. Officer woke with a start, and bolted out from under the covers upon hearing a male voice. At this point everything happened so fast it was a blur. You could've accurately described the incident as "...all hell broke loose!" or "the shit hit the fan!"

Officer flew through the air (and they say pigs can't fly!) and went charging after my friend who was running faster than any cartoon character I'd ever seen. Holding his back, Greg sprinted from my bedroom, booked it through the living room, and hauled ass past the kitchen. Almost to the foyer, I heard him yell something about a "damn pig!" and "I'll see you later!"

I called our vet to discuss these behavioral problems and he informed me that Officer was stressed and overwhelmed with anxiety. *WTF!* HE's overwhelmed?!

"Well, Ms. Volpe, you did name him Officer. He is only fulfilling the responsibilities and expectations you set for him." Again, *WTF!!*

Throughout my incapacitated months, I discovered a few things: Sometimes the people you believed to be closest to you are actually where they are supposed to be—far, far away. And sometimes one person can make up the difference for all the others.

Then there's farm animals, and the power of words. Therefore, I will call my next pig, "Gentleman."

...to be continued

Cooling off on summer days, you will typically find Officer swimming in the waters of Wisconsin.

BROKEN quotation #16

After breaking both of my ankles, I discovered some latent abilities I never previously possessed.

During middle school, I joined junior varsity basketball...and quickly became the team's official *benchwarmer*. Yet, now with two busted ankles and confined to a wheelchair, I am *Most Valuable Player*, with the designated nicknamed, *Lil Lebron*.

Also, I find it ludicrous that I have never been proficient at parallel parking; yet, in my chair, I can turn on a dime and happen to be more precise than a Volvo!

I'm like freakin' Wonder Woman on wheels!

BROKEN quotation #19

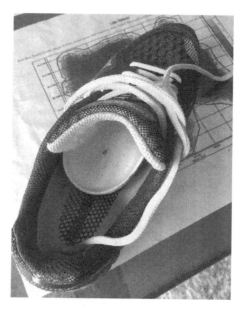

See Lee's shoe...

You know you haven't worked out in a while when you have a spider living in your gym shoe.

...See Lee's shoe with Mr. Spider in residence!

BROKEN quotation #33

When I said I was going to
"make myself more comfortable,"

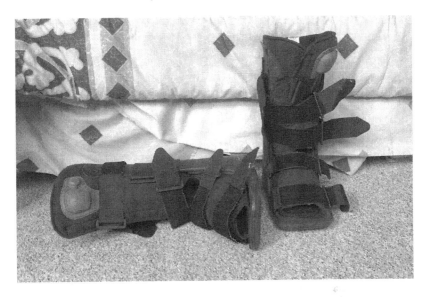

I doubt that me taking off my casts
was what he had in mind...

BROKEN quotation #28

When you are bored at the podiatrist

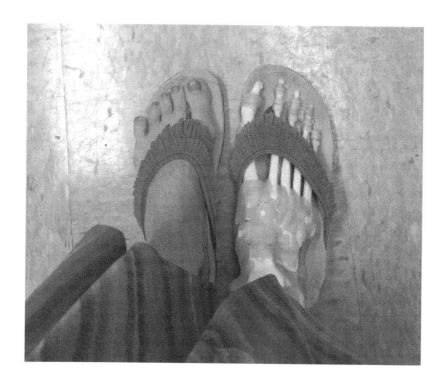

BROKEN quotation #41

It was never about *falling*...
but the lessons learned when *down*
that taught me how to *stand*.

Chapter 5: The End

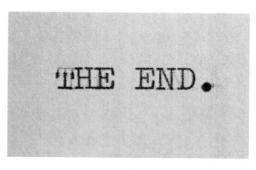

Hello summer, and welcome to serenity!

At the end of June, my mother flew down from our family vacation home in Northern Wisconsin just to drive Officer, Uncle Put, and me back up to join her for the summer. The wheelchair had been returned, the caretakers sent home. I was in two walking casts, and ready to get the hell out of town!

After firing my best friend's company, I also fired him as my best friend. Unfortunately, people I believed to be allies chose sides in the "divorce," and I was left standing awkwardly alone, like the unpopular middle-schooler thinking, *why didn't they pick me?*

So, I was off to Wisconsin—to heal, lick my wounds, and come back stronger and better for it.

Independent July, bee stings, and porn stars—oh my!

 CONNECT   now

You are moving more than a typical Monday.
Slide for more

It's always nice when you receive a text alert announcing you're not being the typical "lazy ass" you've been, and they would be accurate. I was moving more, and every day I was closer to independence. Now if I could just get used to the terrain; walking on rocks, hills, and uneven ground is hard enough with hiking boots, let alone my "boots."

It was the Fourth of July, and the family was all together at the lake. We decided it was the perfect opportunity to take a family photo. My mother, being a wildlife photographer, decided to put fourteen of us in a beautiful field of daisies located on our property. My stepbrother was helping me navigate my way out to my mother's "photo op" destination, when all of a sudden...

Bees! Bees! And me with two walking casts, in a field...and I'm allergic! Yep, that happened. Good news: I can run in walking casts.

225

As I ran back to the house to find an *EpiPen*, my throat began to feel funny, my chest began to pound, and I began to sweat. All of these symptoms could be attributed to the fact that I was running, but I do remember having extensive allergy testing when I was young which confirmed my severe reaction to bees, so I doubted it was the exercise.

By the time I entered the house, the situation had escalated and I was genuinely scared. It took some time searching, but I finally found the injector. Immediately, Officer was on guard. He sensed the severity of the situation and never left my side, snorting all the while. My brother-in-law, the cop, came rushing in to see if I was okay, right as I stabbed myself in the thigh, becoming an official member of the *"EpiPen* Club."

Unfortunately, Officer the mini pig didn't let Waukesha County's finest officer, my brother-in-law, enter.

Ugh, here we go again.

Officer visiting friends during the summer

After the family left the lake house, my mom and I went to decompress and have some laughs. We finished with lunch at a quaint log cabin bar and grill. As we were drinking our beers, waiting for our food to arrive, I noticed the only other patrons were sitting at the bar.

There was an inbred looking fellow in his fifties, with his seventy-year-old mother (or sister, or both!) who served as his wingman. At the opposite end of the bar sat a decent looking man, around the same age, sipping a Pabst Blue Ribbon.

While observing the strange, backwoods pair, things got even more bizarre—but somehow exciting for a small town. The creepy son said to Pabst Blue, "You look familiar—my Ma and I swear we've met you!"

The insignificant guy at the end of the bar turned toward the pair and squinted suspiciously. "You may know me," he said. He finished the last of his Pabst Blue, slid off the bar stool as if he'd practiced it 500 times for a role as an extra in a Western, and headed toward mother/sister and son. As he leaned in next to them, he almost whispered when he said he'd been in movies.

I hushed my mother who was at that exact moment asking me what they were saying. I tuned back just in time to hear Pabst Blue say he was *Lawrence of A-Labia.*

"That's right! See Ma, I told you we knew him."

Ma turned to Pabst Blue/ Lawrence of A-Labia and, nearly swooning, purred, "Well, we sure are blessed to have a movie star in our neck of the woods. Welcome to Serenity."

August, the calm before the—CALM, what calm?!

I'd been deleted by all friends and off all groups on social media associated with my dear old ex-BF. Now I had to go to *LinkedIn* to wish everyone "happy birthday."

And moving on...

I had been religiously doing my physical therapy since leaving Florida. However, my physical therapist in Wisconsin was a bigger pain at times then the exercises.

He asked me how my ankles were healing. I told him they were looking good, but when I said I wasn't sure they'd ever be the same, that they'd become my enemy, he scolded me.

"That's a bad word, calling your ankles your *enemy!*" was his exasperated reply.

Lee's ankle update (Summer 2016)

228

"Huh, no shit...and here I thought *fuck* was a bad word," was mine.

September, my European birthday in Wisconsin...

Happy Birthday to me! I was turning the big 4-0! "I'll be in Rome on my actual birthday!" I breathlessly whispered to myself at least every five minutes in the weeks leading up to the big event—but wait, this is *Lee's Life,* so here we go...

My mother had decided she would take my sister and I to Europe. We would go to Italy and see where my dad's family is from. Then off to Germany to see my mother's side. A quick trip over to Austria, because why the hell not? Have you seen *The Sound of Music*? Well, that's where I was going. I planned to climb every mountain, sing *Do-Re-Mi* on the steps in the *Mirabell Gardens*, and dance around the fountain like the American tourist I would be. But that was before September.

Three days before our trip, my step-dad wasn't feeling well and went to the doctor. Bad News: he had to go to the hospital. Good News: I'm NOT 40 until I get to Rome.

So call *Guinness World Book of Records* because I hold the record of being the oldest 39-year old!

One year ago my life broke apart, little by little. Before my eyes I watched my home, health, and relationships crumble. I was *Humpty Dumpty*, and like *Humpty Dumpty*, I couldn't be put back together again.

...and I am grateful! I am thankful for the ability to gain wisdom, and find the laughter— in "breaking."

I appreciate my independence and good health.

I understand humility. Not many will know what it feels like to be eighty, until they are.

I value what it means to call someone your friend, and how loosely others use the word.

I love myself more, and I love myself most.

AND...I always remember to watch my step.

Summer sunset at the lakehouse
(Wisconsin)

Up North

*Daddy dangling me over the edge of the dock to pee
before a family boat ride.
I'm sure the reason for not permitting me to walk 75ft to the house
bathroom was because this made for a "perfect" photo-op!
(Wisconsin—1978)*

Up North #12: State Symbols

When I was growing up in Florida, we would drive 1,583.8 miles to escape the brutal summer heat. Our destination: Northern Wisconsin and the family lake house.

The Volpe's (a.k.a. *The Griswolds*) would pack up our brown 1980's wood paneled station wagon (yes, a real "Woodie") as soon as school let out in June. My mother, father, sister, dog, cat, cat's sandbox, several tons of luggage, and myself all piled into the car, not to return until August.

Driving north was quite the family experience—and geography lesson. My mom would always have us say *goodbye* to one state, and *hello* to the next. I remember arguing with my sixth-grade teacher about the fact that you can leave the state of Georgia arriving in Tennessee, only to exit Tennessee winding up back in Georgia, and finally re-enter Tennessee and ultimately welcome Kentucky.

Still, once we all stopped fighting, hissing, and barking, I realized: flying was the way to go!

Unfortunately, it was too expensive for our entire family to travel by plane, so I remained in the backseat until seventeen. However, once I left for college it didn't take long before I was earning my frequent flyer miles and enjoying upgrades to *Business Class*. But then Officer, my mini pig, snorted his way into my life, and so now I'm back to being a *Griswold* and driving. Pigs do fly, but *United* clipped his wings; therefore, Officer, my black cat, Uncle Put (*have sandbox and catnip, will travel*), and I all head north in my *2011 Hyundai Sonata*.

Surprisingly, I really have enjoyed the drive. Nothing like when I was a kid in the back of the station wagon, sound asleep on top of all the luggage with the dog!

Sound asleep on a typical family road trip
(Fergie, the Airedale Terrier, & me)

I still say *goodbye* and *hello* to each state along the way and sometimes twice, as we've previously learned. However, these days I find myself reading the billboards, reclassifying each state I'm in by their most repetitive advertisements.

The following is a list I have complied to identify each state from Florida to Wisconsin:

FLORIDA
Strip Clubs and Vasectomies

GEORGIA
Bar-B-Q Pork and Peaches

TENNESSEE
Fireworks and Firearms

KENTUCKY (a.k.a. *Roadkill State)*:
Possibly a few for Bourbon (I couldn't see the billboards through the dead animal bodies.)

ILLINOIS
I *wish* there were billboards, or something to look at!

No, you know you've arrived in this state when everything looks the same and you wonder if it will ever end? It reminds me of being stuck in an incessant game of Monopoly—but worse!

And finally...

WISCONSIN
Cheese and Casinos

There you have it; now you don't need a compass, or even breadcrumbs to make your way north or south.

Just remember, if the state you're driving through is advertising: *Big Daddy's Fireworks*, you're in Tennessee. But...if you find the best entertainment around to be at the *Nimrod Casino Resort,* watching the *Native American Casino Pool Tour Finals*, while eating fried cheese curds, then my fellow road warriors, *Welcome to Wisconsin!*

Up North #5:
Welcome To Serenity

There is a town with only one road in northern Wisconsin; so tiny that if you blink you'll miss it. You know you've arrived on *Main Street* when you see the sign:

Welcome to Serenity!

This unique community has some of the most notable personalities residing within one zip code. I'd like to share a few of the local characters with you.

Tommy Telephone:

Tommy was our town's unofficial White House liaison. My first memory of him is when I was four, and my family and I went to town for ice cream after dinner. The *Main Street Milk Station* was the most popular spot in the area—besides the bar. *Tommy Telephone* was faithfully in attendance every night from five to nine (ten on weekends). It was commonplace to observe comprehensive phone conversations on world affairs between Tommy and the current *President of the United States.*

I should take moment here to mention one teeny-weeny detail...

236

Tommy was twenty-seven years old in 1980, but mentally he was only nine. In 2009, he was still nine. So, now that you are clued in concerning his "limitations," I'll continue...

Tommy regularly let my older sister and I speak with President Carter, President Reagan, and then President George H. W. Bush. My sister was shy, and didn't like talking to most people, much less strangers, but I didn't mind—I loved it! My favorite was Reagan; I remember he had a funny voice and talked a lot about his wife, Nancy. But by the time George W. was in Office, *Tommy Telephone* made a career change to Karaoke.

For the next twenty years, Tommy's one-man show performed the same three songs every Saturday night at the *Main Street Milk Station.*

On a side note, Tommy also moonlighted as a math tutor, although the poor guy couldn't keep a bowling score without calling Thomas Jefferson for help!

Unfortunately, *Fourth of July* weekend (2013), *Tommy Telephone* was "permanently disconnected" when someone ran him over, down on *Main Street,* five minutes after his final performance of *Queen's,* "Another One Bites The Dust."

R.I.P
Tommy

Bob and Brutus:

Bob, the *Wisconsin Wild Turkey*, caught a glimpse of his reflection in a pair of 22-inch shiny chrome rims...and fell madly in love—with himself. He decided to *domesticate*, remaining in the area, just to get one more look at his handsomeness.

Brutus, the proprietor of *Brutus's Treasure Trove, Tires, and Full Service Gas*, was the topic of many town hall meetings. The real problem was that Brutus was a hoarder, accumulating a lot of junk on his property, including his enormous collection of mismatched rims.

Brutus was what you might call "eclectic" in his tastes. He had 1950's appliances and refrigerators, a rainbow of broken-down cars and boats, and a prime selection of *Lay-Z-Boys* from the 70's that had seen more snow than Lombardi himself. And yet, the townspeople complained that his establishment affected the overall aesthetics of community.

The good news for Brutus was that he was the only certified mechanic and service station within fifty miles.

Brutus responded to the local disapproval by befriending a turkey he found loitering, naming him "Bob." and welcoming the bird to *nest* with the rest of his "prized possessions" at *Brutus's Treasure Trove, Tires, and Full Service Gas*. It didn't take long for *Bob the Turkey* to become famous, or as some believed—*infamous*.

During the eight years Brutus and Bob cohabitated, Bob never got over his infatuation with *himself*, or his debilitating obsession with shiny objects. Therefore, when customers pulled in and out of *Brutus's*, Bob would chase after their rims, pecking their tires until they stopped for him to regard his appearance. Even after Bob began the bad habit of *strutting* down *Main Street*, chasing after chrome bumpers, or a flashy pair of 22s, most folk still found him to be "one charming bird." But just like religion, politics, and football, not ALL agree!

Thanksgiving, 2002, Bob was napping in his favorite 1976 *La-Z-Boy*, when a vehicle heading westbound on *Main* was seen driving back and forth in front of *Brutus's*. The man in the gray Ford pickup, with a sticker on his rear window that read: *I Like My Deer Like I Like My Women—HORNY*, had previously been observed taunting and harassing Bob.

Unfortunately, *Bob the Turkey* was duped, succumbing to his narcissistic desires, and was run down on *Main Street*.

R.I.P
Bob

Inbred Fred:

Freddy Gross lived twelve miles outside of town. He looked like Charles Manson's younger brother, and was known for his penchant of "keeping it in the family"—literally! To put it simply, The Grosses were GROSS!

I can't accurately say how many generations of Gross' didn't bother to find mates outside their own tribe, but I can assure you that as far back as my great, great-grandparents, no one in their family has needed to legally change their surname after marriage—which does make things convenient.

Inbred Fred worked at the *Johnson-Peterson Market and Packie* as a stock clerk. Even though Fred didn't own an automobile, nor possess the skill to operate one, he never let that deter him from getting to his destinations.

Fred would attempt to hitch rides down *County Road B* to civilization. Most locals knew him to be harmless, and would offer a lift more times than not. But if a motorist didn't stop...well that's when *Inbred Fred* would misbehave.

Fred would stand almost in the middle of the road, and if it didn't look like you were were slowing down, *Inbred Fred* would hurl himself in front of your vehicle, forcing you to slam on your brakes.

National Siblings Day (2008), Fred was leaving work when he spotted a *2007 Chevy Suburban* rounding the corner. Thumb out, inching closer to the center line and oncoming traffic, he realized the black SUV was failing to slow. Therefore, Fred executed his "classic" move, and jumped...

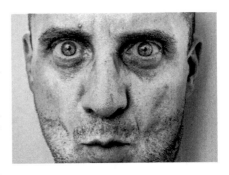

R.I.P
Fred

Unfortunately, *Inbred Fred* was run over by a *FIB* (Fucking Illinois Bastard) down on *Main Street*.

In this little town at the top of Wisconsin, you find *Serenity* on *Main Street;* so beware of the town *dump*; I hear that's where you find *Tranquility*.

Sign at the town dump

Up North #8:
Water Skiing

When I was four years old, I learned how to water ski. On the lake of our Wisconsin summer home, my father "encouraged" me to *not let go of the rope.*

"Just remember: keep your skis together, knees slightly bent, hang on, and whatever you do, don't let go of the rope!"

These instruction where coming from a man who never water skied a day in his life. My dad was from New York, a city boy who was ignorant of the *great outdoors* until meeting my mother and visiting her family home in the Northwoods.

"Hit it," I hollered to my dad, who was behind the wheel of our speed boat, and just like that, we were off,...and then I was down, and underwater, but I held on and didn't let go of the rope.

I was a good girl and remembered my daddy's instructions, but my father wasn't listening to my mother who was sitting next to him, yelling for him to *stop!* Did I mention my dad was hard of hearing and wore hearing aids most of the time—except out on the water?

As I drank the majority of our bay, my father enjoyed the breeze flapping his comb-over side to side and the sun on his face, bronzing his olive skin. Eventually I let go, or he finally stopped, I can't remember for sure. But I did survive his water skiing lesson and by the end of the afternoon, I was successfully skiing around the lake.

Me learning to water ski
(Summer—1980)

The following summer, it was time to learn how to slalom. My mother decided to let the professionals teach my sister and I instead of dear ole dad. We went to a water ski school on the Wisconsin River, and spent the day learning how to drop one ski, balance, and then how to start off on one right out of the water.

My sister did very well, getting the hang of it rather quickly, and was slaloming soon thereafter. I, however, struggled.

I was only five and the instructors said I was too little to do it, that next year I would have more strength and capability. My sister was two-and-a-half years older than me, with legs the length of my entire body—but my dad wasn't accepting any of what the professionals advised.

Early the next morning, my father had us, or rather me, in the water, ready to do the impossible. My dad was someone who, when determined, could do anything, and today that was going to be having me slalom.

Yelling, screaming, tears, and finally...I was gliding along on one ski. It took all damn day, and I was so angry at my dad by the end of it. Another year of ingesting the majority of the lake, and I was already dreading what he was going to teach us next summer.

Unfortunately, we had only a limited number of summers with my father before he passed away. I haven't water skied in several years now, but I still hold the title for *youngest slalomer* on our lake—thanks to my dad's perseverance.

Looking back now, I realize that he wasn't just teaching me how to water ski. My dad was teaching me how to fight, to never give up, to "hang on" and don't let go when life gets rough, but most importantly, to never let anyone tell me, *you can't!*

Yes, I slalom (Age 5)

Up North #50:
Wisconsin Visitor's Guide

Since I can remember, people have always asked, "What is there to do in Wisconsin?" Every summer of my life was spent up north in this state, and my fellow Floridians would grill me with questions  like: "Do you have to milk cows?" "Do you eat cheese all day?" or "What do Wisconsinites do if they are lactose intolerant?" *They mooove to Minnesota!*

For decades I have had to explain the Northwoods to my southern friends. Bonfires, water skiing, Green Bay Packers, haunted houses, Bloody Mary's, and fried cheese curds are just some of the things that come fondly to mind. For those of you unfamiliar with the *Dairyland*, I will introduce you by sharing some state secrets I have discovered, or found interesting.

I'll begin with the most obvious, just in case you didn't know—Wisconsin is the largest cheese-producer in the United States. Wisconsin is also the only state to offer a Master

Cheesemaker program. It takes three years to complete, and you need ten years of cheese-making experience before you can even apply as a candidate. Did you know that the city of Sheboygan is known as the "Bratwurst Capitol of the World?" Cheese, brats, and beer are staples in this part of the country; but what about the beer? (Remember? MILWAUKEE is in Wisconsin.)

Long before Wisconsin became America's Dairyland, it was a bonafide BEER state. German immigrants, pouring into Wisconsin during the mid-1800's, built breweries across the land, and by the 1890's, nearly every community had at least one.

The brewing industry was shut down under the Eighteenth Amendment to the United States Constitution in 1920. Although Wisconsin repealed its laws enforcing Prohibition in 1929, four years before the nation as a whole, the era had already had a lasting effect on the state, leaving only eight-eight operating breweries. Don't cry over spilt beer; the golden hops continue to floweth, but never runneth over.

If you enjoy fairs, there is always Guiness World Record's largest music festival in the nation, Milwaukee's Summerfest. Or, if live music isn't your thing, don't fret, this state has something for everyone. The *Wisconsin State Cow Chip Throw Festival*—the world's largest celebration of bovine fecal matter; some say the entertainment is crappy, but I'll reserve my opinion until I've experienced it for myself.

The city of Rhinelander has its own mythical beastie, the Hodag, which is a sort of horned frog thing. My boyfriend, well, ex-boyfriend, came to visit me one summer

and ate way too many brats, and turned into one (a Hodag, not a brat); I have the picture to prove it!

PROOF!

Unfortunately, Wisconsin was the state that brought us such serial killers as Ed Gein, who inspired films like the *Texas Chainsaw Massacre* series and characters like *Norman Bates*. Jeffrey Dahmer, also a Wisconsin native and notorious murderer, inspired the cannibal, *Hannibal Lecter*.

However, even with all that I have mentioned, the doll, *Barbie*, chose the fictional town of *Willows*, Wisconsin as her hometown. I bet you would have never guess *Barbie's Dream House* was in Wisconsin.

Up North #31:
Go Pack Go!

Only in Wisconsin...

Can you watch the *Packer* game from your emergency room bed, while getting IV fluids for dehydration, with your physician belching outside your room from one too many brats!

Gotta love the Northwoods.

Up North #88:
When Animals Attack

When you think of being attacked in a body of water, most would immediately visualize *JAWS*. Up north, with the cool, pristine freshwater lakes, one never needs to imagine such nonsense.

Being a Floridian, you cannot help but be wary of the deadly critters lurking beneath the water's surface; alligators, poisonous snakes, and sharks—*oh my!* are just a few. Thankfully, Wisconsin is too cold for any amphibious monsters...or at least that was what I believed until the summer of 2008.

I was swimming the shoreline of the lake I grew up on, when ahead of me, I glimpsed a Common Loon underwater. There is nothing "common" about these aquatic beasts, I can assure you now, but then, I didn't deign to care if it was a loon or a lark. I was just surprised to find I wasn't swimming alone.

People up north LOVE loons. I remember when I was a kid, the town would have "Looney Days," when everything was half price and locals would dress up like the beloved bird. You can find *Call of the Loon* CD's, magnets and pins, and *Love A Loon* bumper stickers anywhere, even at the gas station register.

Well, Wisconsin, I don't love loons!

I swam toward the bird and started to follow it rather closely underwater. (Yes, I know, totally uncool to aggravate nature.) Through my mask, I looked into the eye of my prey, and it was RED! Holy crap, it was scary! I froze. I was terrified of a bird, in four feet of water. *Whatever*. Well, I was relieved when it rounded the point, and this time, I stayed put.

Until...

OUCH! I was attacked, assaulted from behind, in my left calf. I had been completely unaware of the loon's mate stalking closely in my wake. He ambushed me, striking with his dagger-like bill. It wasn't long before my survival instincts kicked in, and I remembered to stand the hell up.

I got what I deserved; the lesson learned is *never piss off Mother Nature*. But who knew these beautiful creatures were such nasty bastards?

Google knew, that's who.

Our lovable Common Loon is #6, *Top 10 Birds Most Likely To Kill You.*

Up North #44:
MO-HEE-TOHS!

Summer 2013, I decided to distract myself from my dissatisfying relationship with *the short, bald narcissist.*

Leaving the safety and security of my family's vacation home, I traveled five hours south to my sister's residence, and the "good time" she promised me for the weekend.

Following my arrival, we headed to her friend's house for a day of cocktails, girl-talk, and an overdose of *Vitamin D.*

I remember the initial introductions to her native Puerto Rican friend, and her just as authentic *mojitos;* but everything after that first drink was blurry, and it's probably best to leave it that way... but I won't.

My sister imbibed one and a half, and I ingested two of these *risky Rican refreshments.*

I would later discover her cocktail concoctions contained all the proper ingredients, just not the precise measurements (twelve mint leaves, not twelve rum jiggers). The mint, picked fresh from her herb garden, mixed with sugar, soda, and organic lime juice over ice, somehow camouflaged the half bottle of white rum in each of these lethal libations.

I was having so much fun...until the mojitos began marinating.

Downing the final swig of firewater, its effects flavored my breath and clouded my mind.

From what I recall, the rest of this "good time" went something like this:

I called and broke up with *the short, bald narcissist,* vomited on the Puerto Rican's *Ragwort* and *Rosemary,* unsuccessfully trying to catch it in my red *Solo* cup, and then rinsing its contents out in her pool—because I have manners and was taught to clean up after myself.

Then (I was later regaled with these details by my sister) I managed to get up from my oh-so-ladylike, down-on-all-fours kneeling position by the pool and make my way to the nearest deck chair. My sister was horrified but laughing hysterically as I flopped down and went "lights out."

Hours later, waking up drooling poolside in the moonlight was just as disconcerting for me as it must have been for Dorothy arriving in *Oz*.

Managing to open one eye, I discovered there was actually one munchkin, my niece, Mae, staring down at me curiously.

"Drive me home," I begged her.

I could hear my sister's laughter littering the warm night, and the scent of a non-vegan dinner cooking on the grill.

I knew the signs; we weren't planning on going anywhere anytime soon.

"Mae, help me," I pleaded. "Take me home!"

"I can't, Aunt Lee-Lee," Mae answered.

The world was spinning and I wanted off; I was desperate to get home, so I could die in my own bed rather than my perpetrator's patio chair!

"Why not?" I impatiently demanded.

Concerned, Mae observed me carefully before commenting.

"I can't drive."

"Why not?" I repeated insistently, but with a complaining, whinny undertone.

"Because I'm only twelve, Aunt Lee-Lee."

Two conclusions occurred to me in that moment: Children are absolutely useless. And I have never cared for my sister's friends.

The Benefits of
Birth Control

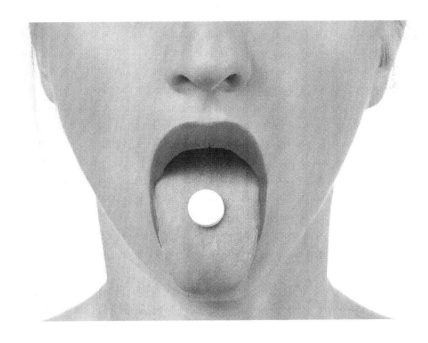

Thank God the First Wasn't the Last

We are going to get very intimate in five, four, three, two...

In high school I fell in love for the first time. My desire to wait until marriage to have sex was quickly diminished as my desire for my beloved grew. The problem was, this is *me* we are talking about, and things are never as simple as they seem or should be.

Ben was not only my best friend and boyfriend, but he was also born with a congenital heart defect known as Bicuspid Aortic Valve (BAV). Now, why would I mention his "defect" in a story about my virginity, you may ask?

Well...

One of the complications of BAV is fainting. Ben never liked the sight of blood, and whenever he saw it, he would experience heart palpitations and loss of consciousness.

So I was not only concerned with a virgin's typical anxieties like: *Will it hurt?* And *Oh God, please don't let me get pregnant!* Or *Am I considered 'easy'?* I also had more serious and realistic fears to deal with, like: *What if Ben collapses and I have to wait for my mother to get home for help?!*

And then...it just happened; it wasn't planned. Many can relate to being swept away in a moment of passion, but can you relate to what came next?

Ben began.

Me: *No, wait; I don't want to!*

Ben stopped.

Me: *Okay, go ahead.*

Ben began.

Me: *NO!*

Ben stopped.

Me: *Am I still considered a virgin if you weren't ALL the way in?*

Ben listened.

Me: *Probably not; might as well continue.*

Ben began.

Me: *OOUCH!*

Ben fainted.

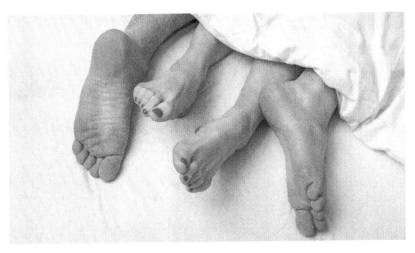

Looking back, it is true what they say: *You never forget your first.*

I am sure Ben never forgot me, as I will always remember him and how thankful I am that he didn't die on top of me.

Sadly, his widow can't say the same.

Last winter, Ben passed out, and then away, in bed with his wife. She said that Ben's final words to her were: *Oh God, I'm coming!*

The Benefits of Birth Control

I used to believe it was more romantic for a gentleman to pick flowers for me instead of buying them,

until one day when...

my date showed up with my neighbor's newly planted Rhododendron bush —roots and all!

Calories Burned In 30 Minutes

Laughing = 40

Sex for a man = 100

Sex for a woman = 69

Banging your head against the wall = 75

A cold shower = 600

What have we learned?

I didn't know my ex-boyfriend

was a philanderer;

I thought he said he was a philanthropist!

Welcome Back, Lee

As the dawn badgered its welcome on my semiconscious mind, I began to accept the reality of another day and opened my eyes. First problem to greet me was that my mascara from the night before had clumped and attached its *Night Navy* ass to my left cheek. Secondly, everything I witnessed out of my right eye was spinning.

Was I Dorothy in Kansas, forever in black and white—or was it sepia? I don't have Toto; I used to have Prozac, my black cat, but now I have Officer, the mini pig. This isn't *Oz*, it's frickin' Florida and I don't have any ruby slippers.

I haven't been lucky in love. I feel like Dr. Seuss': "One Fish, Two Fish, Red Fish, Blue Fish." I almost married my last boyfriend. My gut was screaming from the beginning, but I still excused all those red flags. I didn't know he was a philanderer, I thought he said he was a philanthropist! So now I find myself single again—thirty-something, career-focused, and taking the world by storm.

Welcome to my world. I am sorry to report, dating hasn't gotten any better in the two years that I was confined at home playing "wifey" to a short, bald narcissist. But it could always be worse, right?

Going on a date with a man who describes, in detail, the women he is typically attracted to, when I am clearly NOT his type. Having cocktails, conversing, and then the Latina waitress, not even ninety pounds, with jet black hair to her waist, and deep dark pools of distraction, made this *thirty-something* feel too old in the overcrowded corral of fillies.

My date, *Drive-thru-Boy*, was no longer capable of multi-tasking. I was wrapping up my conversation on how "...I am not a jealous person, unless you give me a reason...If you're staring at someone else and I have to wipe the drool from your face, that would be a problem for me...", when he saw *Señorita Valentina*. Five minutes later we were in the car, on the way back to my house where he dropped me off, never having eaten dinner—nor did he walk me to my front door.

Once inside, I immediately walked to the garage, got in my car, and drove to the corner *McDonald's* for a quarter-pounder with cheese and large fries. And large vanilla shake, of course. As I turned the corner and pulled forward, you will never believe what I saw. *Drive-thru-Boy* was in the line two cars in front of me!

He called the next day wanting to do dinner and a movie. *Seriously?!* Is it answer enough when you would rather stay home doing your taxes?

Dinner after work with friends at the local Italian eatery became ridiculous once my status returned to single. The owner, Vincenzo, kept trying to set me up with his cousin Lorenzo, a twenty-seven-year-old pizza maker who needed a green card and didn't speak a lick of English! Vincenzo had to translate the introductions. When Lorenzo asked for my phone number by handing me his cell, everything was in Italian. I had to laugh...and politely refused to put in my number. Lord knows what Vincenzo told Lorenzo since he hardly spoke English himself. However, Lorenzo looked hopeful, smiling profusely, repetitively regurgitating *Si* over and over again. At least *NO* is universal!

Officer is always putting a dent in my dating life, too. Any man that tries to get close to Mommy, he charges. The short, bald narcissist left an impact on my pig as well.

Needless to say, "When life throws you a curve ball... DUCK!"

Therapists are like vibrators...

every woman over twenty-five

should have one

—whether they admit it or not!

Latin Lovers

I always know when I have gained weight by the reaction of men.

Typically, my fellow Caucasians stop flirting to make room, not only for my ass, but the line of ethnic men.

The following story is just one example that proves my point.

I was walking into a *7-11* around lunchtime, when this young white guy walking out almost knocked me over—as I held the door for him!

While inside, I encountered a group of migrant workers who didn't speak English. My Spanish is minimal, even after four years of it in school. All I can actually say is, "I have a headache," which does prove useful.

As I rounded aisle two, I encountered one of the laborers. Now, I am five feet, three inches, and my little amigo's forehead was barely level with my chest—which was probably part of the problem. The other problem was his lack of communication due to the language barrier; so how do you flirt?

I'll tell you what my Latino admirer did.

Barked! Yes, the man barked at me by the Jack Link's Original Beef Jerky.

So what does any nice, slightly plump, classy white girl do? Hiss!

**To avoid unwarranted advances
from a suitor,**

**do as I do and start a fight with
your imaginary friend over
whom he thinks is prettier.**

**If that doesn't do the trick,
excuse yourself so they can be alone.**

Dick Doesn't Live Here Anymore

"Is Dick home?" My neighbor's eight-year-old grandson was back for one of his visits...and looking for my ex-boyfriend, the short, bald narcissist.

"We discussed this last time, Noah. Dick doesn't live here anymore."

"Why?"

Why had been Noah's favorite word for the last three years; I finally had to admit, Noah was a little "special."

I tried to explain, for the umpteenth time, that I broke up with Dick, and Dick hadn't lived here for almost two years! It seemed Noah was having just as much trouble understanding this as the United States Postal Service.

"You got divorced?!" Noah replied with a shocked and worried look upon his cherub face.

Oh, boy. "No," was all I simply said.

I knew that Noah had a keen knowledge of automobiles and immediately fell in love with Dick's luxury ride. Dick, however, did not fall in love with Noah's red BMX racing alongside that "luxury ride."

"Do you miss Dick, or do you miss his car?" I asked Noah.

"Why?" he asked. Of course.

"Well, I remember Dick wasn't very nice to you. He yelled at you and made you cry," I reminded him.

"Why?"

I continued without pause. "You got too close to his car one day with your bike, so he screamed at you, and you rode off in tears."

"Well, that wasn't very nice!" Noah almost yelled with indignation, as if hearing this for the very first time.

"No. Dick could be [a dick] not very nice," I said.

"SOOOOOOO, when will Dick be home?" Noah

looked up at me from behind red handlebars—and was serious!

I did the only thing there was left to do. I looked down into the deep blue eyes of my neighbor's eight-year-old grandson...and I lied.

"Dick died," I said sadly.

The only time I have ever been dumped by a boyfriend was on April Fool's Day.

As he proceeded to breakup with me, I kept laughing, saying,

"HA...April Fools!"

Betsy Jo Cobbledick

Betsy Jo Cobbledick was a good Baptist girl when I met her during my freshman year of high school. Obviously, she had an unfortunate name, especially when she had her friends call her B.J. instead of Betsy Jo.

B.J. was more than a little naive when I met her, but when she came back after summer break, she had drastically changed. While she had been away at Youth Camp, B.J.'s parents separated. However, Betsy Jo had other concerns, namely, how to develop the ability to get the attention of boys.

At good ole Baptist Youth Camp, B.J. lost her virginity to a young, handsome youth pastor named Abraham. She later met Adam, then Bartholomew— but after Caleb, she believed it was God's *will* for her to only sleep with men with names from the Bible— and her OCD (Obsessive Compulsive Disorder) insisted it be alphabetical.

I moved away my Junior year, and by that time B.J. Cobbledick had a reputation of a gutter snipe, to put it nicely; I saw her more as a misguided soul.

Whatever happened to her? I had heard through the years that B.J. had worked at the Atlanta *Boom-Boom Club* instead of going off to college, but then settled down, had a family, and was doing well. When I moved back to the area, I was overly surprised when I ran into her.

Wearing skin tight shorts with her butt hanging out (among other things), blonde, lop-sided pigtails, and twin boys, one on each hip, she greeting me in the *produce* section of the local grocery store.

Three more of her children, all under the age of eleven, were causing havoc, running loose around the supermarket. I was able to keep track of them by the latest "clean up" loudspeaker announcement; at the moment, they were in aisle five.

As I returned my attention back to B.J. and her life story, I couldn't remember if she said her third husband was Samuel, or did she say it was Timothy? No, she and Timothy only dated. Goodness, Betsy Jo Cobbledick had been a busy lady since I had been gone.

"Zechariah is my soul mate, the one I've waited for my WHOLE life," she announced enthusiastically, jostling one son around on her hip, and then rearranging the other boy.

"Well, that's wonderful; I'm so happy for you," I kindly stated.

I mean really, what could I say?

"You know it's never too late, Lee, you could still find that special someone," she encouraged.

"Listen B.J., the last guy I dated was Andrew. I have a long way to go to get to Zechariah—and I've never been overly religious."

Can the mother of two boys and a girl please come collect your children from the Customer Service counter. Again, can the mother of three children IMMEDIATELY come collect them from the Customer Service counter. Thank You!

Ah, saved by the blaring announcement.

I haven't seen B.J. since that day at the market. Sometimes I've wondered if she is still madly in love with Zechariah, and what will she do if she's not; who is *left* in the Bible for her to date?!

Then I recalled there's a sequel to the Old Testament. Matthew, Mark, Luke, and John are among many in the New Testament, and I finally understood the true meaning of *God's abundant love.*

Driving one day when I happened to look up and see this ...and it made me happy.

You know you live in a small town when

there is no one left to date,

but your ex-husband!

Dominatrix Dating Dilemma

I happen to know of two guys whose "bromance" reminds me of *Oprah* and *Gayle King* (television personality, magazine editor, and morning news anchor—a.k.a. Oprah's BFF). Most have heard of these iconic sister-friends of over forty years, but you have yet to meet their male counterparts.

Let me introduce you to Mike, who I call *Oprah* due to his booming voice, captivating presence, and empathetic nature. Whereas Matt favors *Gayle*—the tall, slender side-kick, who alone is brilliant, but disregarded in the company of their celebrated crony. These BFF's have done everything together since meeting in 1986 at a Bon Jovi concert in Baltimore, where they were seated together, sang tunelessly in unison to "Livin' on a Prayer," and bonded over a passed joint.

A regular fixture in each other's family photos from that point on, they had been roommates in college, dated twin sister's in their twenties, co-founded a lucrative online business in their thirties, and now in their forties, their friendship still hasn't abated. To prove this point, I will share a particular story from last month when these two double-dated a pair of local dominatrixes. (Incidentally, I am one of those people that others always confide in; people seem comfortable sharing anything and everything since they are confident I am not a blabbermouth—forgetting of course that I am a writer and it could end up in my book.)

One day Oprah met a professional dominatrix by the name of "Lady Wanda Whiplash," who just so happened to have a protégé, "Svetlana Sinstress," for Gayle. It was a slow week with all the snowbirds returning north for the warmer months, therefore the girls were available to meet for drinks on Saturday night.

An exciting, educational evening for these boys abruptly ended their cocksure swagger when their dominatrix dates joined them for a nightcap back at Gayle's place.

Lady Wanda led Oprah to a back bedroom and shut the door. Svetlana, being the perfect understudy, followed her Mistress' lead; dragging Gayle to the master bedroom, she shut the door behind them.

The guys had been informed that the *safe word* was: "There's no place like home." If either submissive, Oprah or Gayle, wanted to signal "stop" during the session, all they had to do was say: "There's no place like home."

The guys, always willing to try something new, didn't allow their ignorance with such bedroom play dim their enthusiasm.

Until...

"THERE'S NO PLACE LIKE HOME, THERE'S NO PLACE LIKE HOME!"

In unison, echoing from one side of the house to the other, the boys firmly invoked their *safe word*.

Poor Oprah had stiletto heel welts all over his lower back and buttocks, and Lady Wanda Whiplash's panties caught in his dental bridge work. Still, he was doing much better than his buddy, Gayle.

Svetlana Sinstress, the beginner, was yelling at Gayle to "Bark like a dog!" while hitting him over the head with a wooden hair brush; after suffering from a relentless headache, he was later diagnosed with a mild concussion.

Battered, bruised, a visit to the emergency room—and dentist, was just another adventure for these two. However, I do believe their one and only date with these dominatrixes left an impression. I happen to know this because one of my favorite movies is *The Wizard of Oz,* and whenever Dorothy speaks those famous words, *There's no place like home,* Oprah hysterically bursts into tears, while Gayle begins barking like Toto.

For a good time,

call...

someone else.

Hear Me Roar

"You need to get practical. Fairytales and falling in love isn't realistic at your age. You're getting too old for all that, and it is time to get serious before it's too late."

"For Christ sakes, Daddy, she's only 30!" my mother said in defense of my grandfather's heinous spiel.

My love life, or lack thereof, had been the topic of discussion over countless meals with family. As my grandfather sat across from me, loving concern muddling his features, he unsuccessfully tried explaining what he meant to say, while I drifted back to only a year ago when I had spoken about my desire for marriage and children. And he, HE had told me I was too young to be thinking about all that nonsense; I had plenty of time! I should have realized then. After all, this is the same man who faithfully excused my weight, insisting my chubbiness was just "baby fat"—at 30! (I promise you, it is no longer baby fat.)

That was almost ten years ago, and though not much has changed, I've changed. The anxiety I have experienced as an unmarried, childless woman has been overwhelming. For all you *attached* readers, let me be the first to explain what it's like to walk in my size-6 *Jimmy Choo's*. (Okay, so it's more like size-7 *New Balances*, but that's beside the point.)

Today, society says it's *acceptable* to be a strong, independent, single woman—well I say that's a bunch of hooey! Maybe if you are a lactating narcissist, but if you are smart, attractive, and breathing, you are a societal enigma. I'd like to see a survey from a reliable source confirming tolerance, because I'm regularly regurgitated with offensive questions like: "Are you married?" If I'm not married then: "Do you have a boyfriend?" If I'm not seeing anyone, then: "She must be a lesbian."

Snow White serenaded seven dwarfs with a song about how, *Someday My Prince Will Come,* and hers did; whereas mine doesn't have a GPS and is too stubborn to ask for directions. I know there is nothing *wrong* with me, and I don't want to be typified or put in a box; yet there is an undeniable stigma attached to my *single status,* and miserably I found myself not only agreeing with the masses, but accepting their estimations.

It was time, past time to reimagine life after *Prince Charming* failed to show up on his white horse. Now that my *eggs* have almost expired, and I have yet to put my "big breeding hips" to good use, the likelihood of not being a biological "Mommy" has been difficult to accept. I resigned myself to the reality that my niece will most likely get married and have babies before me. At this rate, so will Caitlyn Jenner.

Is that what happiness IS—marriage and children? Am I not fulfilling my legacy as a woman? Am I shunning my natural obligations?

My internal voice was fed up and ready to revolt. Mourning the loss of my unborn children, I found strength in women who never wanted the title in the first place, and their full, limitless lives. I feel liberated and inundated with endless possibilities. I don't believe in fairytales anymore, but I do believe in superheroes—and I'm ready to kick ass! So, don't allow others to judge your worth by the *suit* standing next to you; focus in on yourself. I'll buy my ticket in the marriage lottery, but when I do the stakes won't be so high because I've taken this time to get to know myself. And by the way, I AM happy! Why should it take someone else to make me whole when I already feel complete?

If you really want to know who I am, watch me, because I lead by example. Hear me, because my voice is wise and honest, and I speak loud and clear.

Touch me and feel my strength. Know my heart is brave; my love—pure and unconditional. Hold on, because I am a catch, and I need no one to be relevant. I am a daughter, a sister, an aunt, a friend. I laugh, I cry, I stand tall at 5 feet, 3 inches high. I am a woman, I am not just one thing; don't label me. I am HER, I am SHE, I am US, I am WE—but you may call me Lee.

Me (2013)

Happily Never Afters
With Aunt Lee-Lee

The *Real* Princesses of Never After

Sleeping Beauty was not the lazy, depressed princess we all believed her to be. Afflicted with severe *sleep paralysis*, the poor thing was plainly suffering from undiagnosed narcolepsy.

As for the Prince...CLASSIC Necrophiliac!

Now, Rapunzel was just uncultured and unkept. If a guy can crawl up inside your hair and get lost, you have seriously just one-upped Howard Hughes!

Still, Snow White was by far the worst. *Heigh Ho, Heigh Ho*, was actually: *High Ho*. Thanks to an incessant cocaine craving, this lily-white princess' reputation for bartering her "apple bottom" in exchange for *snow*, was the biggest scandal since that walking *fish stick* (a.k.a. The Little Mermaid) flitted into the kingdom.

The Seven Dwarfs didn't help to muffle gossipmongers, considering they were NOT extremely short, proportionate beings with a growth-hormone deficiency, but rather the possible symptoms of poisoning: bashful, happy, dopey, sneezy, grumpy, sleepy—call the DOC!

"Skin white as snow, lips red as blood, and hair black as ebony," Snow White might have been *fairest of them all,* but nevertheless, she was still one bad apple.

Red In the Hood

Here is the real story about our dear Little Red Riding Hood...

When Little Red was just a baby, her folks, Father Hood and Mother Hood, perished in an unfortunate accident. While taking the short-cut home through the dense forest, the Hoods lost control of their rig as a wayward wolf in sheep's clothing crossed their path, killing them instantly. Regrettably, Red was raised by her paternal grandmother—and Granny was nuttier than a squirrel's turd.

By age 6, Little Red was tasked with supporting Grandma's sweet tooth; by 18, she was uncloaking in the *hood* and riding the pole, while selling her candy-coated treats on the south-side.

Little Red regularly wandered the woods to Grandmother's house, delivering baskets full of sweets. One particular day, while lying in bed in the throes of withdrawal and awaiting her next fix, Granny heard a knock at her door. It was not Little Red Riding Hood.

Did I mention they called Red "little" because she had a height disability, and stopped growing at 4'7"?

Anyway, when Red ultimately arrived, she was startled by Grandma's condition, "What big eyes you have..."

Her grandmother's features resembled a wolf's; the swollen, puffy appearance, and labored, panted breaths positively spooked Red, until...Granny died—undiagnosed type 2 diabetes.

Unbeknownst to Little Red Riding Hood, the Notorious B.B.W. (Big Bad Wolf) had visited Grandma's house earlier that day with a deadly dose of Krispy Kreme.

That was the true story behind Granny's death, and inevitably how the Big Bad Wolf got his reputation as a real "lady-killer."

The Adventures of A Little Wooden Boy

Once upon a time, there lived an old Italian woodcarver named Geppetto...and his little wooden puppet.

The truth was, Geppetto experienced a serious reaction from taking the prescription drug, *Cialis*. When his *wood* lasted longer than four hours and wouldn't go away, he neglected to seek medical attention. Instead, he named it Pinocchio.

That's the real story; trust me, I wouldn't lie!

The Frog Prince
a.k.a. Cold Sore Croaker

The *Frog Prince* is the most disappointing damn story. The youngest and prettiest of the King's daughters loses her stupid gold ball that she endlessly played with in the forest. I think it is fair to conclude she may also be the village idiot.

Incredulously, a talking frog comes upon her, offering to find the missing treasure if she agreed to be his friend and take him home. Giving her word, she anxiously awaited the croakers retrieval and return. Gaining her golden globe, she grasped it tightly to her chest, and in a flash, she fled the forest...and the thwarted toad.

Eventually, the Frog Prince showed up at the castle gates. Disappointed in his daughter for breaking her promise, the King demands that she fulfill her end of the deal. Next thing you know, there is a jumping amphibian dining and sleeping with the princess, per Daddy's orders, until *Day Three,* when he miraculously turns into a Prince and marries the beautiful village idiot.

Seriously? What kind of polliwog poop is that?

The modern-day tale goes something like this:

Don't be the village idiot, taking home and kissing just any frog, or you'll wake up with mouth herpes— NOT Prince Charming and a marriage proposal!

Hindsight 20/20:
Wicked Stepmothers, Goblins, and Other Fairytale Meanies

Tonight, on this edition of Hindsight 20/20, *we investigate the lives of famous fairytale children, the evil suffered at the hand of their guardians, and the truth behind their classic tales.*

Child Star #1: Geraldine Locks (a.k.a. *Goldie Locks*)

Born Geraldine Locks (preferring to be called, *Goldie*), this gal was a natural entertainer, performing since the day she was born. Goldie Locks was discovered at age nine when she was crowned, *Junior Miss Apple Blossom of Arlington Heights.*

With an overly ambitious stage-momanager, having aspirations of her own, Goldie was well on her way to stardom. Typical of most fabled child-stars, Goldie Locks was considered a "washed-up, has-been" by her eighteenth birthday.

Neglected by her momanager who was vacationing in the French Alps, bizarre reports of Geraldine (a.k.a. Goldie Locks), currently homeless, frequently dominated the daily headlines.

Labeled *Hollywood Hoochie Mama* by most, never knowing whose bed she's going to crawl out of, seemed minor in comparison to her recent troubles. Reliable sources have emerged claiming Goldie was found at Soldier Field, *squatting* in the men's locker room during the *Bears'* off-season!

We will continue to cover and regularly update you on this breaking story.

Child Star #2: Hansel and Gretel

These poor kids! Imagine having a stepmother who was like: *We don't have enough money to take care of your children, Honey. So, why don't you take them to the middle of the forest and leave them there.*

Their bona-fide *deadbeat* father agrees to child abandonment methods rather than getting a job delivering pizzas for the extra cash.

After THREE attempts at ditching his children deep in the woods, this Deadbeat Dad was shocked when little Hansel and Gretel managed to find their way home each and every time—even after being held captive by a crazy witch who wanted to eat them!

However, upon arrival from their recent hike home, they discovered their wicked stepmother had suddenly died...and NOW this *single* father was happy to have his baby's back home. Sounds rather suspicious, don't you think?

We will continue to monitor and update you on Hansel's and Gretel's future whereabouts.

Child Star #3: Mr. Miller's Daughter

Everyone gets all caught up in the name, *Rumpelstiltskin*, when the real story is about poor Mr. Miller's daughter.

Heinously, Mr. Miller, an impoverished brewer, sold his youngest, most beautiful daughter to a wealthy, powerful man (said to have made his fortune in debt collections, but my sources have not confirmed this). Miller's outstanding promissory notes, plus his drunken gossip of his daughter's "gifts," enticed the gluttonous gaze of this perverted *repo man*. Unfortunately for Mr. Miller's daughter, her befuddled father signed an immoral contract stating that if she did not bestow her bountiful *gifts*, she would pay with her miserable, inconsequential life.

Ensconced in the attic upstairs, Mr. Miller's daughter anxiously anticipated the coming evening, and the expectations of her master. Amazingly, a little person abruptly unlocked the door and then, pushing it ajar, ambled in. (Yes, yes, the little man was Rumpelstiltskin—an *Amber Alert* waiting to happen.)

Agreeing to his stipulations for assistance, Mr. Miller's daughter quickly outsmarted and outmaneuvered the mythical dwarf. You see, Rumpelstltskin had his name written in the back of his tighty-whities; after first guessing, *Calvin Klein*, naturally her next answer was correct.

Rightfully, she succeeded in gaining her freedom, not only from the crooked contract drafted by her *repo ruler*, but from the German goblin with an unhealthy baby obsession. Unlike our pervious fairytale children, Mr. Miller's beautiful daughter DID live *Happily Ever After*. Presently, she and her child have since moved to St. Louis, where she is married to a young, up-and-coming Master Brewer named Bud Weiser.

That concludes this edition of, Hindsight: 20/20, *but tune in next week when we examine the boy*

who could fly, but was incapable of growing up—Peter Pan: the Manolescent Inspiration Behind the Syndrome.

Muther Goose

Mother Goose was one sick *muther*!

While everyone complains about the "youth of today," let's dig deeper into the teaching tales of their earliest educator—a deranged, dysfunctional duck.

Mother Goose has been telling her stories and rhymes to children since the 17th-century, but did you realize this country bumpkin was a full-blown racist?

Baa, baa, black sheep

Have you any wool?

Yes sir, yes sir, three bags full.

One for the master,

And one for the dame,

And one for the little boy

Who lives down the lane.

Poor *Baa, Baa* had to give its wool to the "master," but Mother Goose doesn't stop there; no, this greedy fowl wants to go after the competent Mr. Woodchuck, and all of his chucked wood.

Did you ever before think about Mother Goose's propensity for preaching child neglect and abuse?

A wonderful example is the nursery rhyme, *Rock-a-bye Baby.* Some suggest it was written by a pilgrim observing the way Native-American women rocked their babies in birch-bark cradles suspended from tree branches, while allowing the mother to work freely knowing her child was safe from animal predators.

Sure, put a helpless infant in a tree, let the wind rock it around, and when the branch breaks, we'll all sing together as the baby falls to the ground.

And what about the *old woman who lived in a shoe?*

There was an old woman who lived in a shoe.

She had so many children,
she didn't know what to do.

She gave them some broth without any bread,

And whipped them all soundly
and put them to bed.

This irresponsible single mother had too many children, and was suffering from a dreadful bout of postpartum depression. So much so, that she starved her kids and beat them soundly to sleep.

~~~

The one thing Mother Goose does not do is discriminate. If you can assault the children, you can surely abuse and murder the parents...like *Peter Peter Pumpkin Eater*.

Peter, Peter, pumpkin-eater,

Had a wife and couldn't keep her;

He put her in a pumpkin shell,

And there he kept her very well.

It is believed that Peter's wife was a hooker, whom he couldn't keep from her indulgences in tricks or treats, so he killed her one Halloween and put her body in an absurdly large jack-o-lantern.

Thanks Mother Goose, for telling future husbands that if their wives get a part-time job, become unfaithful, or just don't obey, you can kill them and stuff them inside a giant squash.

Having poultry as a parent is obviously not the wisest influencer of adolescent minds. Discovering this *domestic* geese's penchant towards prejudices, her incompetence as a babysitter, and an impaired ability to problem-solve, it should come as no surprise when I share a secret about two of her delinquent prodigies.

Jack B. Nimble was a hyperactive pyromaniac who burned down his mother's house jumping over a candlestick. He is currently uninsurable, taking the prescription medication, *Ritalin*, and fulfilling his community service sentence advocating ways of preventing forest fires with the National Park Service.

Lastly, good ole *Georgie Porgie...*

> *Georgie Porgie, pudding and pie,*
>
> *Kissed the girls and made them cry;*
>
> *When the boys came out to play,*
>
> *Georgie Porgie ran away.*

Well, everyone should know that *pudding AND pie* is code for *going both ways*. Georgie, who was rumored to be the lover of King James I, was also a sexual harasser and womanizer, notorious for deflowering half the kingdom. Today, Georgie would be a registered sexual offender.

~~~

So, parental guardians of the world, do you want this *muther* raising your chicks...or should we cook this goose?

Acknowledgments

I would like to recognize and sincerely thank:

Dr. Arnold Z. Schneider (my therapist): who helped me grow into a happy, healthy adult...into a person who embraces her *true self*...into someone capable of discovering and implementing the humor of any situation, and the ability to SEE in the DARK—all for under $200 an hour!

Joe Jacobson (Words and Writers): without whom I would never have had the ability or skill to launch a professional website and blog, nor the opportunity to meet my publisher and traverse this new road I'm on. You have been a guide, teacher, and social media resource; I appreciate your support—and patience.

Barbara Dee (Suncoast Digital Press, Inc.): who has "humored," mentored, as well as encouraged me throughout this process. Your editing and manuscript preparation help was priceless! Thank you for always grounding me with your calming, peaceful way.

Just your typical Sunday text message to my publisher

Marsha Friedman (publicist) and the entire *EMSI Public Relations* team:

*The book has arrived and it's time
to absorb and digest the
Celebritize Yourself Method
from the master herself, Marsha Friedman.*

I am wise enough to know the value in having a professional team like this on your side; you can't help but go places—and soar.

Thank you for representing, advising, and navigating lil ole me.

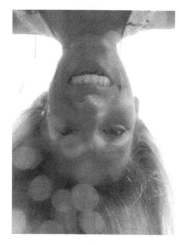

Lastly, I would like to remember all the *Assholes* for the many stories they have inspired. Without whom, this book would never have been possible.

XO, Lee

Credits

H photography
—Cover and photo on page 44.

Arielle Original Art
—Photos on pages ix, 2, 24, 43, 129 and 306.

Dan Malavich
—Photo on page 226.

Dreamstime

iStock Photography

Shutterstock, Inc.

All childhood photos provided by
the Volpe family archives

A writer will never stop writing.

Only when there are no words left

will the story end.

About the Author

Lee Volpe (Wisconsin 1979)

Creatively writing since childhood, Lee Volpe has never been at a loss for words. After a short career as an actress, Lee found her voice as a humorist, and has never looked back.

Since 2011, Lee Volpe has been making a name for herself professionally as an honest, Laugh Out Loud (LOL) humor writer, dealing with daily life and relatable situations. Applauded for saying what most are thinking, Lee has the unique ability of finding wit in the way and amusement in the angle.

Lee Volpe
(Author Profile Picture)

Erma Bombeck meets Sex and the City
—Marcia Corbino, Herald-Tribune

Currently dividing her time between the Suncoast of Florida and Northern Wisconsin, this *SWF* shares her life with her two boys: a black cat called Uncle Put, and a miniature house pig by the name of Officer.

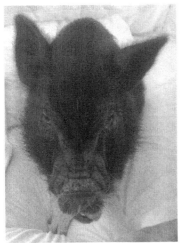

Officer the Mini Pig
hogging
my king-sized bed

Uncle Put anticipating my slumber,
...and his ultimate destination
—my head!

To learn more, go to:
LeeVolpe.com
...where laughter begins

Note from Publisher: Expect a 2018 release of a must-have book, authored by Officer the Mini Pig.